I0089459

STRONG Mom
STRONGER Daughters

LIVE LIFE WITH GRIT & GRACE

SHERRI HILTON

Copyright © 2023
Sherri Hilton

Performance Publishing Group
McKinney, TX

All Worldwide Rights Reserved.
All rights reserved. No part of this publication may be reproduced,
stored in a retrieval system or transmitted, in any form or by any
means, electronic, mechanical, recorded, photocopied, or otherwise,
without the prior written permission of the copyright owner,
except by a reviewer who may quote brief passages in a review.

ISBN: 978-1-956914-55-9

CONTENTS

Introduction - It Takes a Leap of Faith. ix

Relationships - Happiness Begins with a Wink and a
Smile–For Yourself and Others. 1

Make you a Priority - Putting Yourself First Is Not Selfish . . 9

Money - Work for It Until It Can Work for You 21

It's Not About You. 29

No Excuses!. 37

Ice Cream Smiles for Decades to Come 47

Mastering Your Mindset Matters 55

Be Vision Driven and Goal Focused. 65

Happiness Begins with a Wink and a Smile -
"Co-inky-dinks" 75

That Little Voice Inside You 83

You Had Me at Hello.. 89

Laying Low and Accepting the Status Quo Is Not
Okay–EVER!. 99

**It's important to me that I leave behind the
strength that was given to me by so many
women who came before me.**

Thank you to my biggest supporter, cheerleader, voice of reason, the
one who will listen to all of my crazy ideas and have me believe I am
capable of even my wildest dreams – my mom. The quiet lady who has
been by my side since birth, who taught me to be the strong woman
I am today. Thank you for always being there and pushing me to
complete this project. I'm beyond grateful for you and blessed to have
you as my mom. God sure picked the best mom a little girl could ever
have in you.

To my girls, Charley and Dani. I want you to grow and become the
strong women I know you are capable of being. I hope that I have shown
and continue to show you how to be independent women who can do
anything you put your mind to but are soft enough to allow the right
people in your life to be by your side along the way. Life is better with
someone to smile and enjoy it with, which is why I'm grateful you have
given me memories that will last a lifetime. Thank you for cheering me
on during this passion project. I hope my lessons are your step stools
to achieve more out of life than I could ever dream. "Dream big, bold,
and boundless" – you are capable of more than you know.

I can't forget about those Vickieisms and the light they shed on the
world as my Aunt Vickie did for so many. I only wish she could be
here to know how much they have impacted, guided, and enlightened
me throughout the years. I don't know how many times I would sit
to write in silence and catch myself talking to her or listening for her
voice. Even though she is not here next to me, she has been with me for
every step and word of this book. I have drawn wisdom, intuition, and
guidance from her, and I hope you feel as if you are her friend when I
talk about her and her Vickieisms. 'Til I see you again…

The cover of my book and journal are drawn by my friend Amy Lee. I
firmly believe in "co-inky-dinks" and that paths cross for a reason. Amy
is an incredible artist, but never shared her talents until one night on
Facebook. She casually shared one of her paintings for the first time,

and it stopped me in my tracks as I was scrolling. This image spoke loudly to me, and I just knew it was what I wanted for the cover of my book. I was so afraid to ask her and hear a "no," but I got up enough courage one afternoon, and I'm so grateful I did. Always remember, it doesn't serve anyone to keep your talents to yourself just as much as it does not serve you to not ask for what you want, because of fear of rejection. Step out and share your gifts; you have no idea who you may touch.

Thank you to Beth Graeme for my photo on the back cover. If you are ever in Southern Maryland and need a personality photo shoot, professional headshot, senior portrait, family photo shoot, or any photography, give Beth a call. You will not be disappointed. Beth also volunteers countless hours for Gals Lead, a non-profit organization in Southern Maryland that helps to empower teen girls to embrace their full potential. This group is truly inspirational and acts on women supporting other women, raising them up, and mentoring youth to live with a greater purpose.

Thank you to Michelle Prince, my publisher, for believing in me, encouraging me, providing feedback, and getting me to the finish line. You are special, and I am so glad our paths crossed when I took that last-minute trip to one of your workshops. There are times when you can see the lines marked on your life's timeline… when events happen that change you forever. That event is marked for me as it was a turning point in my life when I found myself again. The workshop and year of coaching with you and Howard Partridge influenced me for the better. I thank you and wish you so much success and happiness in life.

As Aunt Vickie would say, "Love and Light."– Sherri Hilton

INTRODUCTION

IT TAKES A LEAP OF FAITH

Y ou are not alone. So many people—women, in particular—
put on a strong front so it looks like they have it all together.
I know from experience. Many people, even those close to me, do
not know some of the struggles and experiences I've had that I've
kept to myself. I have always been viewed as strong, successful,
put together, attractive, smart, "the one who has it all together."
Need I go on? But the truth is, while my life may seem perfect on
the outside, I have had to deal with many challenges. There have
been days I could barely hold it together. You've probably had those
days too. Days you just want to open up to let out the person on
the inside so everyone can see the real you.

We are all broken in some way, and it's in the brokenness we
heal and begin to find ourselves and the true calling God has for us.
My latest struggle left me as a single mom with two little girls. Now,
I know I'm not the first single mom and I clearly won't be the last.
Deep inside I know I've got this and can handle whatever comes
my way. There is a strength and force greater than me looking over
and guiding me along the way. I know I'm here to raise two little
girls to be strong women who can tackle anything in life, can stand
on their own, and—most important of all—are happy. I tell my
girls all the time, "God gave me two hands for two little girls." I'd
go through the last seven years all over again to have them.

The setback of a failed marriage motivated me to write this
book in the hope of helping not just my daughters, but young
women and single moms everywhere. This is what I want them
all to know:

"You can do anything you put your mind to. You already have
inside of you what's ultimately needed to make anything you
want out of your life. You just need the courage and support to
take that first leap of faith to change your life forever."

We all have choices, and with our choices come consequences. It's how we use the lessons that can make the difference between moving forward and sliding back. Our mindset is powerful, and we must look for the blessings and learn from our past so that we do not repeat it.

Dani, my younger daughter, tells me all the time that she was put here to make me laugh. I can't imagine my life without my two little girls. But I must raise them to be stronger than I have ever been, so that they do not repeat the same mistakes I've made, and instead, take on a life better than the one I have.

It's not easy raising girls these days, but it is our job and main purpose to help get our children to heaven. I believe God gives us more than we can handle because he wants us to rely on him at times. There have been so many low days in my life that I have struggled. When I turned to him and gave it over, knowing he has my back and I am not alone, the path became lit, and I knew where to go. We can do anything with God's grace and his sacraments. It's time. As Mary Poppins says, "Walking around in a fog.... You're too focused on where you've been to pay attention to where you're going."

It's time to look ahead, learn from the past, and reach down with a hand to pull others, including my daughters, up. It is my mission to show them my struggles so they can learn from my mistakes; I want to instill values that uphold what it is to be a respectful, strong woman. I want them to do better than I have and to know that they are children of God. God has big plans for their future, plans he has already set in place. He also has big plans for you! My girls are here for a purpose, just like you and I are.

It is my hope that this book will encourage, guide, and, ultimately, show you how to embrace this crazy life with all of its challenges; how to become the strong woman that I know we are all destined to be. It's taken me quite some time to have enough courage to put words on paper and allow people into my life to see the imperfections, but I firmly believe these imperfections were put there to help others— as well as myself—heal.

We all have struggles. We have all been in situations we look back on and wonder, "What was I thinking?" Sometimes, the thing you feel was going to break you into pieces will be what makes you realize who, and whose, you are. Your struggles may be just the thing to show you what you are capable of, and that, my friend, will be worth more than you know—to you, and to those around you who are watching. We need to pull ourselves out of the struggles, learn the lessons, and then help others to not repeat our mishaps.

I didn't think it would take me this long to find myself again, as strong as I seem to be, but I'm glad I finally turned the corner. It just makes me sad knowing how long it may take others who do not have the outlook or resources in life to get themselves through the darkness. It is my mission to make sure my girls have the best outlook possible to help them through the rough times.

Isn't that what we all want? Encouragement? I'm here to tell you that "perfect" on the outside isn't necessarily perfect on the inside. Some of our biggest struggles give us the greatest growth. Through our failures, we learn and do better the next time. It's time to get over some of the struggles, grow as a person like you've never grown before, and raise your daughters to be strong women. Even if you do not have a daughter, you are a role model and influence for women and young women around you. Your advice, lessons, and successes can help them in more ways than you realize. Women need to support, encourage, and help each other.

I've been very blessed to have strong women in my life. At a very young age, I was taught and told many times by my mom,

"You can do anything you set your mind to." I firmly believe this and now I teach it to my girls. Nothing is ever out of reach. I can tell you from experience, I've had failures, money issues, toxic relationships, loneliness, death of significant people in my life, breakups, divorce, illness, unhealthy habits, and fear, but it's the struggles that show you what you are capable of.

One thing I know for sure is that I've learned from my past, and with those lessons, I'm doing my best to teach my girls so they can handle whatever life throws at them. There will always be ups and downs in life. Think of an EKG and the peaks and valleys it shows as the little dot flows across the paper in rhythm with your heart. This is your life in a picture. It is my hope that you draw strength from the highs to get you through the lows. It is my hope we will all learn the lessons that our past can teach us so we don't have to repeat it. Trust me when I say, if you do not learn the lesson, the next test is even harder until you finally get it. My Aunt Vickie used to casually remind me of this.

I lost my very dear Aunt Vickie a couple of years ago. Talk about strength. If she had an idea in her mind, nothing was stopping her. She taught me so many ways to look at life a little differently. My mom used to think we were crazy when we got together and would talk about manifesting life, visualizing, and "co-inky-dinks" (coincidences). I will never be able to repay her for what she taught me, but I know it's my obligation to teach it to my girls. I miss Aunt Vickie's talks and her presence, but I know she is with me every day.

One day, still feeling lost from my divorce and the loss of my aunt—let's just say it was one heck of a year—I happened upon a webinar. It was for a book conference with Michelle Prince. I knew I had to be crazy to just jump in and go for it only a week before the conference, but looking back, I can't imagine what my life would be like today if I had not taken that leap. Something about the webinar intrigued me. Was it Michelle and her connection to Zig Ziglar, whose work I had studied and read so much in my past? Was it the fact that writing a book had always been on my goal list? Or maybe it was just the fact that it was in Florida in January, because there's nothing like the warmth of the Florida sun in the middle of winter and having lived in Florida for almost a decade, it has the feeling of home!

I asked my mom if she would watch the girls, used reward miles for my plane ticket, and didn't look back. I had felt so "off-path" for several years, but there were so many things that happened during those three days in Florida that weren't just coincidences. Besides, as Aunt Vickie would say, "There are no co-inky-dinks." The people, the energy, and the events put my life into motion. There are times when life lines up with the right people and events you can feel the synchronicity in the air. You know at these times, without a doubt, God had a hand in connecting you with the right people and life starts to easily fall into place. You have to be open and willing to see the possibilities, say yes to what comes your way, and connect to those around you.

Before I left, I signed up for a group that would become a big part of my life. The group: Two Peas in a Pod. Two coaches: Michelle Prince, a publisher who had worked for Zig Ziglar for many years, and Howard Partridge–author, business owner, and exclusive small business coach for the Zig Ziglar Corporation. It was Ziglar's book *See You at the Top* that started my sales career many years ago. Mr. Ziglar was an incredible and inspiring man whose work has motivated and encouraged millions around the world. With the help of Michelle and Howard, I "found" myself again that year. I reconnected with the person I once was, but who had been lost for so long.

I have taken many of the lessons I learned over the years and have put them on these pages to help and inspire other women to know that anything is possible. Share these lessons with your daughter, niece, or even that young girl who looks up to you. You can instill values that will help form amazing, strong young women.

Back to my dear Aunt Vickie for a moment. I talk to her quite often. At times, I can feel her presence. I know she is with me—by my side with a smile and a chuckle because of what's about to come to life in these pages. Her essence is scattered throughout this book. I hope you use the words to strengthen your life and the lives of your daughters and young girls whom you will impact from this day forward. May this book create a ripple effect to begin a movement, because I know this world can always use more strong moms and stronger daughters. Get ready—it's time to take a leap of faith.

RELATIONSHIPS

HAPPINESS BEGINS WITH A WINK AND
A SMILE-FOR YOURSELF AND OTHERS

F amily and friendships are the most important and valuable relationships you will ever have in your lifetime. It is necessary to step up to be there for them because one day you may not have the opportunity.

I was living in Florida in my early 20s. I had finished my undergraduate degree, purchased a house, and was working to complete my master's degree. My parents had assumed I would return to my home state of Maryland after completing my undergraduate degree, but I stayed in Florida and started building my life. Since I'm an only child, I'm sure my parents wished I had come home (and now that I have children of my own, I know how they must have felt). Yes, we got to see each other on holidays and occasional visits, but I look back now and see that I missed out on almost a decade of great memories with my parents during some of the better years of their lives.

I was away when my dad built a new house for my mom, and I missed nine summers that could've been spent on his boat fishing the Chesapeake Bay. I can never get any of that time back. You do not realize at a younger age how much those times will mean later in life. I know my life would have been totally different had I not moved from our small town and county to go out and grow, but I can't help but to think of the years spent not being close to my family.

A couple of years after I finished my MBA, I started to get strange gut feelings about my dad. I kept asking my mom if he was ok; I wondered if any of his earlier medical issues were returning. My mom kept telling me everything was fine, but the feelings and thoughts in my head would not leave me alone. As a matter of fact, the feelings would sometimes make me sick to my stomach. I finally spoke to my employer and asked if I could work from Maryland and travel for work from my parents' home

for a month or so. I did just that in hopes that it would ease my mind to know all was well.

Once I arrived in Maryland, events in my life somehow began to flow and I found myself there permanently. A letter arrived out of the blue with an offer to purchase my house in Florida for much more than I had paid for it, so I packed up and moved back to Maryland, knowing I could find another house in Florida if I needed. I took a chance and opened a salon to generate additional income since I was only working when I traveled for my job. The process of opening the business went smoothly. It's amazing how when you are on the right path, doors open, and life flows easily. That's synchronicity and I learned how to take notice of it. My Aunt Vickie taught me all about learning to pay attention to the signs and especially when the co-inky-dinks are lining up and life starts to happen for you in the most synchronistic ways.

I was meant to move home when I did. The business? It provided me an income when my dad did become very sick later that same year. I was able to help take care of him without losing my job/income. Owning a business allowed me to take him to appointments, be by his side, and care for him over the next three years. Those three years were some of the hardest I have faced as a daughter and only child. That time in my life serves as a constant reminder that family and close friends come first in life. The job or career will always be there, or you can get another one, but your family can never be replaced.

As I write this, tears are streaming down my cheeks, remembering the days during those three years that I would not trade for anything. The memories and the time spent with my dad will live in me forever. The laughter, car rides, delivering crabs to the doctor when we visited the hospital in D.C., sitting in waiting rooms, spending Christmas in the ICU, taking him to dialysis,

picking him up for the first time to get him in his wheelchair, the crazy truck he bought that was low to the ground to help us get him in and out easier—I wouldn't trade any of it.

My mom and I are so close, and she is a huge part of my girls' lives too. She gets so much joy spending time with them and making memories as a family. I know these times won't last forever. It's important to make sure to store as many memories in our "mind vaults" as possible.

Always take care of your family, be it your parents, spouse, children, siblings, or close extended family because one day they may not be there for you to spend time with, and I can guarantee that you will regret not taking the time. Time is one thing we will never get back—make sure you do what you want in life and make sure those around you know you love them and how much they mean.

On Christmas Eve 2016, I got to tell my Aunt Vickie I loved her, and I got to hear the words back that she "loves me more." That, by far, was the best Christmas gift ever as it would be my last with her before she passed away. We spend so much time preparing for special days or events, trying to make them perfect, but at the end of the day, it's about the people we love and our relationship with them. My time with others isn't always perfect by any means, but I'm so grateful for the time spent.

Second to your immediate family is your church family. You should have a church that you feel is home when you walk through the doors. Your friends there, as well as the priest, will serve as a parish home when you need spiritual hugs, prayers, guidance, and support. It may be in church and with your church family that you will learn about and get to know Jesus. You may also get to know him in your own personal quiet time of prayer or Bible study. It's important to have a personal relationship with

him. He wants to hear about your day. When was the last time you pulled up a chair to sit and talk with him?

When you form and foster a relationship with God, you will be amazed how your life will open up. You will feel a sense of peace, and you will learn to hear his voice as he speaks to you. These talks will help you know you are on the right path; they will guide you to the plan he has for your life, and best of all, they will remind you that you're never alone on this journey. He is listening and wants to have a relationship with you, but so many people do not take the time to pause and start to form one. When you have a spiritual relationship in which you pray, thank God for his many blessings, and open up to his purpose for your life; you will feel a strong sense of calm and gratitude for everything you experience and, especially, for the people in your life.

Then there are relationships with friends, mentors, and coaches. Be personal and get to know those in your life that mean something to you. Who doesn't love to get to know people, hear their life stories, learn about their goals and dreams, and feel like you are part of a community? In our house, there is a basket that sits on our kitchen table in which there are all types of cards, envelopes, and stamps. It is a little way to teach my girls to connect to people in this crazy digital world of being connected but still feeling so alone. When they want to thank someone, wish a friend a happy birthday, say congratulations or apologize, encourage someone, or say get well—whatever message they want to convey—they can grab a card, write a special note, and drop it in the mail. How awesome do you feel when you get a handwritten and mailed card today? It's way better than a mailbox full of "adult life" bills–I can attest to that!

Everyone wants to feel special, and it's up to each of us to help form and nurture the relationships that mean the most to us.

These relationships are the ones that will be there to encourage you on your rough days, cheer you on in your successes, wipe your tears away on your sad days, and support you on your hard days. These are the people who will keep you accountable to your goals and dreams and be by your side with raised arms and smiling faces when you achieve them. Those are the relationships and friends to surround yourself with. If the friends you have don't do this, or they are not supportive, positive, or encouraging, and are not there for you, then may I suggest finding a new group of friends.

You need to have persons of positive influence in your life—people who will challenge you and become role models in some area of your life. It's important to have coaches and mentors you can learn from, to whom you can be accountable, and who will push you to limits you never knew were possible. You and your goals are affected by your surroundings. Associate with big thinkers—those whose thoughts are bigger than your thoughts. They will influence you in ways you won't understand at the time. The energy and mindset of these people, and the relationships that are formed, will shape your life.

You are like the five people you hang around the most. Find people doing things you want to do, in careers you want to have, with values that align with yours and similar goals and dreams for life. It's easier to achieve and accomplish the goals in your life when you know it's possible because someone you know has done it. It's easier to tackle those goals when you have a group of supporters who encourage you.

There will always be a group of "friends" who don't always have your best interest in mind. They will watch you and what you are doing in life; they will talk to others about you; they will always be the ones with doubts and questions. Be ever so careful

of these friends and learn to recognize them in an instant. It's ok to have these friends, but make sure to let what they say go in one ear and out the other. They are not your true friends and do not have your best interest at heart.

It's so easy to get caught up in our digital world of "likes" and comments of "friends," but I find those are not the same and cannot replace actual relationships and surrounding yourself with some great people. Unfortunately, "friends" on social media can sometimes be negative towards you because they do not know the real you or your intentions. These relationships can sometimes be superficial and lack depth. Keep in mind that those who talk about you, put down your dreams, have negative things to say, and question your motives are the same ones who will be the most surprised when you prove them wrong. When you achieve your goals, they will want you to show them how you did it and will have a change of mind about you. Some may still be negative toward you and say what you worked for was given to you or that your success must have just been luck. It's probably why I've always had the motto, "You say I can't do something? Watch me." I wish I had an easy "friend detector" to pass along, but over time, when you focus on yourself and your personal growth, the distinction between real and fake friends becomes easier to see.

Even though your circle of five may change many times throughout life, always have close relationships that you can count on through the good and the bad times. Those friends, coaches, mentors, spiritual family, and actual family will be the ones you make memories with and remember special times. They are the ones to look forward to spending time together, knowing there is so much more to life than just work and a routine. Make the most of your relationships–Happiness begins with a wink and a smile.

MAKE YOU A PRIORITY

PUTTING YOURSELF FIRST
IS NOT SELFISH

Most women put others first, care for everyone else around them, and go out of their way to help in so many ways. As a woman who has learned the hard way, I will tell you to make yourself a priority. If you don't care for yourself, you're useless. Nothing will matter until you are taken care of, and you know who you are, and your worth. You will be useless to others unless you are whole. It's hard to love others when you don't truly feel the love for yourself. There will be times when you will put yourself last. After getting married and having children, I would always push myself to the bottom of my to-do list. It took me many years to learn that if I had only made a little time for me and had not lost myself in everyone else's needs, I would have been more balanced, healthy, and happy.

I encourage you to pause in the times when you push your needs to the bottom of the to-do list. Pause and look in the mirror. If you are not happy, relaxed, and healthy—or if you just don't feel good about yourself—you will be giving off the wrong vibes to your children and those around you. Kids know when Momma is unhappy or not feeling good about herself. Just as Dani tells me, "Mommy, it's time to go see Harvey and let him paint your hair."

Find yourself a good hairdresser, esthetician, masseuse, and fitness trainer. Don't be afraid to hire a life coach, see a therapist, or find a mentor to show you the way toward your career goals. Make sure you take time for a hobby to keep some passions alive as well as some quiet time for rest and reflection that is good for both the mind and body. Focusing and working on you is necessary at times.

There have been a few men in my life whose friendships have lasted a lifetime. These men have been there on days when I really needed a pick-me-up. They have made me feel like a million bucks in just a couple of hours. They have squeezed me into their schedule even when it was last-minute, and I was in dire need. They have always asked how my day, week, or month has been. They have listened and offered advice. They have pampered me and made me feel like a queen. They have eased my stress and calmed my nerves when life was crazy and I needed to escape.

When I say I wouldn't trade these lifetime friendships for anything—I truly mean it. When I moved back to Maryland from Florida in my mid-twenties, I would return to Florida to visit one of these men a few times a year. Sawn was one of my favorites, and I miss him dearly. He made me smile every time I saw him. He was a happy, fun loving, down-to-earth, older, gay man. He invited me to travel to Paris and Greece with him one summer during my college days. To this day, I regret not taking that trip. He would visit Paris to get medical treatments before heading to his home in Greece to spend a month to relax, continue his medical treatment, and recover before returning to the States. As I look back, I realize what an amazing trip that would have been! To be on a Greek isle with someone who really knew his way around, who knew the people and the culture—that's a once-in-a-lifetime offer. (Side note here: when adventures present themselves, take the trips, the chances, the risks. In my view, it is much better to just take the leap and figure it out than to look back one day with regret—God's got you!)

A few years after I moved back to Maryland, I got a call explaining that my friend's health had taken a turn for the worse, and he had passed away. They called to tell me because they knew how close we were and what he meant to me. Finding someone to fill the void he left was not easy, but my girls have met his "replacement" and love seeing him, even at their young age. His name is Harvey.

Sawn was my hairdresser in Florida before Harvey came along. If I were to add up the years these two men have been with me, it would total over two decades. That's longer than almost anything else that has been a part of my life. There is nothing better than leaving their hair chairs feeling like a new person on the outside. You certainly do not need a man for a hairdresser, but these men have helped to make me feel beautiful on the outside, when some of my days were not so bright on the inside. Taking time out for yourself to get pampered, a quick trim, painting those greys, and out the door can do wonders for you how you feel.

Gregory gives amazing facials. A good esthetician removes the bags under your eyes that can come from all those sleepless nights caring for a baby. They can put back the moisture you lose when you're dehydrated or not eating right (because you are always on the go and are the last one to sit at the dinner table and eat–if you eat at all). A "Gregory" will make you look bright, well rested, and ready to conquer the day after he wipes away the last few months or sometimes years of buildup from that face of yours. This can also be done on your own at night or one afternoon while you relax with your cup of tea. Taking time to take care of your own self, spending quiet time relaxing, and keeping up with your health will not only benefit you, but those around you.

James is a beefy former Marine I have nicknamed "Killer James." He and I have a love/hate relationship. He tortures me in his spin and workout classes, but I wouldn't have it any other way. I owe part of my 40-year-old body to "Killer James." He motivates me, pushes me to my limits, and gives me a fist pump with a smile at the top of that imaginary mountain I just biked. What do you do daily or at least a few times a week for your physical health? As a mom, you need to make the time for your own physical health and well-being. You have little eyes watching. With more and more online fitness classes, it's now easier to turn on a class when you can fit it in your schedule without ever leaving your home. You don't need a Peloton or fancy equipment; you can use apps with your own bike or simply step outside for a walk and some fresh air. I constantly have to remind myself on my busy days and extended busy weeks or months, to just take 30 minutes for myself to do some physical activity. If you are not physically healthy, you are definitely of no use to anyone around you.

I wouldn't replace these friendships and habits for anything. I encourage you to find some of your own rituals that are your go-tos for your self-care and make you feel special. I totally understand that all three of these men are working on the "outside" of me, and it's really about how I am on the inside, but I don't have to tell you that when you feel good about what's on the outside, your confidence is multiplied on the inside. So many people are self-conscious of certain things. Maybe for you, it's your teeth and smile, or your weight; maybe it's a speech problem. Whatever it is, if it makes you feel self-conscious, please do yourself a favor and work on ways to make it better. I want you to always feel your best, be happy, and smile. Find a team who, like "my men," will help you on those days when you need a pick-me-up or simply a "refresh" on the outside.

Self-care is also allowing yourself to be well rounded and whole. I know I'm a better mom because I'm a *working* mom. I try not to dwell on the time away from my kids. I don't stress over the lack of time available to volunteer at school or how many class parties I can make it to. I have two little girls who know Mom works hard to earn money to provide for our family. When I am able to volunteer at their school or pop in for a class party, it is even more special to them. I do make the time for field trips, field days, and recitals. I am at their sports games, and you will typically find me on the sidelines of practice with a laptop in hand so I can catch up on my workday to make up for the time I took out to run them around.

Women multitask as if it is a trait given to us all at birth. Multitasking can sometimes be to our detriment and is often not as resourceful as we think. I'm starting to learn how to "time block" my days. This allows me to focus on one task at hand, knowing I get a block of time to work on my next to-do. Not only does blocking time give me the ability to focus on what is directly in front of me, but my mind is not feeling stretched in different directions because I know I have time blocked for all of my items that day.

Our minds do not work well when we feel like we have 12 tabs open and that little icon is circling. You may just accomplish more in a day if you take a few minutes to prepare your top three must-do items at the beginning of each day. Take that quiet time each morning to prepare your busy day, feel grateful for what you have been given, and look at your vision board to know what direction you want your life to head. Our lives are so busy that we can lose focus on our priorities, direction, and goals with all of the daily noise. Taking time to prepare your day, block time for tasks, and choose what to focus on can put you in the right mindset for those obstacles that may be thrown at you.

It's important to show you are productive at work. You may not always enjoy it, but do your best at whatever you choose to do. My daughters know Mom strives to be the best at her career. They have watched me set goals for our "Champions Club" or "Presidents Club" award at work, and they've seen how I have crushed those goals. The smiles on their faces—and knowing I've modeled for them what's possible when you set your mind to it—well, that's worth more than any trophy I've ever won.

My work achievements and awards were not possible on my own. Supportive leadership and great teammates can make all the difference. When you are looking for a career or position within an organization, the manager and your teammates are just as important as the role you are seeking. Most of us spend 40+ hours a week working. Yes, we would all like to get to a shorter work week, or work for ourselves thinking it's easier, but even in these cases, you are still spending 40+ hours a week being productive to earn income. It's easier to love what you do and be successful if you have leadership with encouragement and a team that supports each other. As with a personal trainer to help me in my physical health, I've sought out mentors and business coaches to help guide me in the direction of my career path and goals. Find out if your employer has a mentorship program or a career path to help get you where you want to be in five or ten years. As a woman in the corporate world, it's important to seek out supportive women who are in the position in which you'd like to be. They can give you insight and guidance from their experience—a road map, if you will—to make your path a little easier than the one they followed. Learning from their mishaps or mistakes without experiencing them can save you time and energy. Mentors and business coaches are more important than you realize.

Find yourself a hobby. Try not to lose yourself in motherhood. I was at a bridal shower for my cousin the other day and we played one of those bridal shower games where we guess favorite things about the bride. She's a young mom of two little girls under the age of four, who works in healthcare, and is looking forward to married life. The question—what is her favorite hobby? As we waited for her to shout out her answers, this one stumped her. She said, "I'm not sure I have one anymore as I'm a busy mom and they take up my time."

We have all felt it. Being a mom or not, when we do not prioritize ourselves, our needs, what brings us joy, and what makes us smile, it goes to the bottom of our list when there is no time left in the day. Putting yourself first is not selfish. Taking time for a hobby you love like photography or painting can help relax your mind from the stress of the day and will bring you joy. What fills your heart and makes you smile? Do more of that. What are some of the things you enjoyed doing before your days got full of kids, sports, homework, meals, packing lunches, bedtime, sick days, kids' birthdays, and being your child's Uber? When I think back, I can see that for so many years, I didn't have a "me." What does that show my daughters? What does that teach them? Does it tell them I'm not worth the effort? That I don't value myself or have a life outside of them? I've come to find that my girls are so happy when they see me enjoying life, doing the things I like to do, and on occasion, taking the time to live life outside of our immediate circle. Like my kids, yours probably do things on their own and have their own individual interests. They have hobbies, sports, activities, and things they look forward to. Why shouldn't you?

Be an advocate for your health. No one knows you better than you do. Being healthy is important for you and your family. If you are not healthy, you can't enjoy doing life with them, and you might not live to be present for them in the years ahead.

Health is one of the top things I neglected when I first became a mom. Lack of sleep left me delirious. Sleep is so important for your brain to function. Your brain needs to rest after an active day. Your brain needs to go through the stages of sleep so you can awake refreshed and ready to take on the day. In the first several years of motherhood, not only was I lacking sleep, but I was lacking any real *quality* of sleep. I can remember climbing into the back seat of my car in a parking garage—outside a client's building—and taking a power nap in the middle of the afternoon. Without it, I just couldn't finish my day. Plus, I knew when I got home, my second job of being a mom would kick in.

Top producers and other successful people are more likely to work out five times a week, but that's hard to do if your body hasn't been rejuvenated by a good night's sleep. Once you have the sleep issue resolved, figure out what to do to get—or stay—in shape. You don't have to go to the gym to work out. There are many options for working out at home these days. You can simply take a walk around your neighborhood or run laps around the ball field while the kids are practicing. (Yep, I'm that weird mom doing laps around the kids' ball field.) You might be surprised how good you'll feel after a workout. Your mind will give you a hundred excuses not to do it, but I promise, if you will push yourself to do something active, you will thank yourself later. Hormones released when you exercise reduce stress and make you feel so much better! Remember, you are showing your daughters that it's important to take care of themselves physically in order to live a long and healthy life. You only get one body; you need to take care of it both inside and outside. Do it for yourself and do it for the young girls who are watching you—and taking notes.

Make yourself a priority, and see how much more you have to give when your glass is full. The saying goes "You can't pour from an empty cup." Make sure to fill your cup first. Flight attendants instruct passengers to "Put the oxygen mask on yourself first before helping others with theirs." If you are running on empty due to lack of sleep, unhealthy eating—or barely eating at all— and lack of exercise, how in the heck will you be able to care for the little ones who are depending on you?

Show your family you value yourself, and watch life fall into place. You are not only helping yourself, but you are showing your kids how to do it so they can look back one day and say, "Mom always made time for herself, so somehow, I can too." Stop the guilt, ladies. You shouldn't feel guilty for giving yourself time and attention. You didn't lose yourself when you gave birth, you became a role model for the "mini you" you've been given to raise. Today, love yourself enough to make you a priority.

MONEY

WORK FOR IT UNTIL IT
CAN WORK FOR YOU

Oh, how I wish my parents had taught me more about money at a young age. I remember them sitting at the kitchen table with all of the bills in a pile and picking out one or two that would get paid that month. My dad was always buying some new "toy"—be it a motorcycle, boat, or antique car. My mom was the one with the steady/normal job, and my dad, well, he would "hustle," as he liked to call it. He owned his own business all his adult life and somehow made it work. He was able to bring in money to cover the necessities like food, electric, water, a place to live—and his expensive toys.

On the other hand, I would visit my great grandfather who owned a shoe store and lived in a huge townhouse in northern Virginia—in what is now the upscale McLean and Vienna area close to Washington, D.C. When I visited Granddaddy, he would take me to the country club where I would help him drive the golf cart, and he would visit his "lady friend." Granddaddy kept $10,000 in the trunk of his new Cadillac, a few thousand under the cushion of his office couch, and on a bookshelf in his office were stacks of silver dollars.

Two very different viewpoints of money. Both influenced me greatly. I would learn and grow from them both—the good and the bad.

Fast forward to college. I had earned two full scholarships—yes, full rides with room, board, and tuition. I also had one partial paid scholarship. But I had no concept of money or just how lucky and blessed I was to receive not one but two full rides to college. One year into college, my independent-self decided to transfer, move out of state, change majors, give up all of my scholarships, and pay out-of-state tuition on my own.

I had to use college loans to live and pay for school—because of their financial habits, my parents didn't have money saved to help pay for my college education and quite frankly it should not be up to them to pay for my college. No one showed me how to save or invest money so I could put myself through college. When I did graduate—also earning an MBA—I had accumulated just over $50,000 in student debt. (I hate to think how much higher the cost for a degree is today, not to mention a Masters.) But here's the kicker: I also had more than $27,000 in credit card debt!

A look at my spending during that time makes it clear I had no money sense. Clothes, trips, eating out: you name it, I bought it. On the plus side, I did own a house I had purchased when I finished my undergraduate degree, so I guess some of the credit card balance was used for home repairs and other house-related expenses. But geez! I felt like I was ten years old again, except instead of it being my parents at the kitchen table with a pile of bills each month, it was me.

I then read a book that would forever change my perspective on money: *Rich Dad Poor Dad*. I quickly learned the difference between a *need* and a *want*. For the next month, I accounted for every penny, writing down everything spent–down to the cup of coffee or sweet tea I bought on the go. I learned about the "latte factor"–how that $5 cup of coffee five times a week would cost $1300 a year. I learned really quickly where the holes in my budget were and where I could cut back to start paying off the credit cards.

When the bills came, I would play a game with myself to see if I opened one that was the larger payment or the lower payment. I felt like my parents at the kitchen table picking bills and realized I had not learned about money the right way growing up. It was painful as an early twenty-something, living on my own, having that much debt and making multiple payments each month, but I had done it to myself.

I had to get my spending under control before the student loan payments began, or I would never be able to make ends meet. After my month of research—counting every penny to see where they all went—I started cutting back in every way I could. In just over a year, I paid off $27,000 in debt, and I have not looked back since.

What's my point? Debt will cripple you. You will feel like less of a person, and the stress alone will feel like an uphill battle. Credit cards are a no-no unless you pay them each month in full. Large purchases should be made with cash if at all possible. Some debt is ok. If you're investing in real estate or in a business or if you're investing in yourself in a way that will pay off later, then debt can even be good, but be wise when making your spending choices. If you can learn a few things and teach them to your little ones, maybe they'll see that Mom knows best, and she wants what is best for them.

With that in mind, here are some lessons for you:

- Always think about whether the thing you want to purchase is a true *need* or a *want*. It's ok to have wants. We all have wants. But you can't spend all of your money on wants. And you never, ever charge a want unless you can pay it off the following month. Needs are different because, well, they are things you need.
- Keep your spending in check. After I did my month of research, I continued tracking every expense. I learned QuickBooks, and it may seem like overkill, but I still enter all of my spending each month. I can tell you down to the penny how much I spend on food, utilities, clothes, eating out, my nails and hair, even what I spend on the

dog. There are some great apps out there now that can be a great tracking tool.

+ Invest in yourself first. It's important that, if you work for someone who offers a 401k match, you put in the maximum amount of money your employer will match. It's free money, why would you even think to turn it down? Before working for an employer who offers a 401k, you can open a Roth IRA that earns tax-free interest.

+ Save, invest, and donate. I know it sounds simple, and I've tried to teach my girls at a young age, but you'd be surprised how impulse buys or wants will sometimes creep in and you think, "Hmmm, just this time." If you're investing in yourself first (401k, IRA, stocks, real estate, etc.), saving for large purchases (or those wants), and making sure to donate along the way, I'm sure you'll be on the right track with little left over to get yourself in trouble from spending too much. You will get to a point, when you see your money grow, or watch what compounding interest does; that you get excited to invest in your future. Stick to your budget and know you don't always have to keep up with the Joneses. Sometimes not eating out, but rather enjoying dinner at home with friends and family ends up being more entertaining than that fancy dinner in a restaurant.

+ Always have six to nine months of living expenses available for unforeseen situations. Then, you'll always be in a good spot if you need to suddenly leave your job, pay for a huge repair on your house, or face an unexpected emergency. I left my job suddenly in Florida because I was miserable. I knew I would be ok for a bit because I had some money on the side. I didn't have six months of living expenses saved, but I knew I was capable of bartending to make ends meet until I could figure it out. We will talk about it in another chapter, but don't let work be work. If you're unhappy, and you dread getting up every day, please make sure you always have a "Leap of Faith" account on hand so you'll be able to walk away and find your happiness.

+ Investing. I've explained that it's important to pay yourself first for 401k, IRA, and stocks. But you may also want to look at things to invest in that will provide you with an income stream or dividends later. It's important to learn about passive income and compounding interest at an early age. Look toward your future as having your money work for you. Passive income is taxed differently and at a much lower tax bracket. You pay more tax on earned income you have to work for. At some point in your life, wouldn't it be nice to have more passive income than earned and be able to take life slower so you can enjoy raising your kids or spending time with your grandkids? Real estate, owning a business, rental income, and dividends from stocks provide passive income. Writing songs or books pays royalties. There are so many options to have your money work for you while you are off working or even while you're sleeping!

+ Giving. It's certainly not last on my list. I've just saved the best for last. Having all the money or things you want in this life won't be worth it if you're not helping others get what they want and need. I've hopefully taught my girls over the years, and continue to show them, how important giving back is. I write a check weekly to our church family. I see our church as our home, and it's important to contribute to our home monetarily. But we also support other programs to help those less fortunate—food drives, Thanksgiving dinner boxes, angel tree projects at Christmas, and so on. Outside of church, there are endless possibilities and opportunities to give.

+ You can give to your kids' school by volunteering. It doesn't cost you a dime, but the time spent is so appreciated by both the teachers and your children. My daughters absolutely love seeing me at school and being a part of their lives in more ways than just at home. We've made "poor bags" together to give to the homeless, and we've substituted birthday presents with donations to the animal shelter and local Veteran's home. We've also gone to the senior center where we visit the elderly and sing songs. There's nothing better than volunteering and giving back to pick up your spirits. Whenever you are having a bad day, take an afternoon and find somewhere to volunteer or help. It will change your life perspective, and trust me when I say, you will get way more out of it than you will ever give.

IT'S NOT ABOUT YOU

I 've done my best to instill in myself and my girls a mentality of looking out for others and to always be mindful to reach out to help them when you can. I will tell you that nothing will give you more satisfaction than helping someone else. Help can be in the form of stepping up and being there when they are in need of tangible things, but it could be many other ways as well. It can be helping a classmate with homework or studying. It can be listening when someone needs an ear. It can be reaching out to the one person who always seems to be left out and alone. People need each other, but some are not included, not chosen, teased, and made fun of.

We live in a world that lacks verbal one-on-one communication. It is easy to quickly tell someone HBD in an abbreviated form and move on to the next thing. Don't do it. Take a moment for those you truly care about and tell them how you feel. It means more today than ever before because it seems to be so rare. Even if those you care about do not reach out to you, reach out to them anyway. Sometimes they don't do it because of the busyness of life, but if you play by the same rules, eventually the relationship will die.

Friends are hard to find and even harder to keep. Be a friend who is *there* for others, because life can get pretty lonely when there's no one to share it with. I pray that when you see someone who has no one, you will step up and shine your light. Many of the roads on life's journey are difficult, and you never know what another person is going through that day, week, month, or even year.

We all struggle. It may be an illness, a death, verbal or physical abuse, PTSD, anxiety, depression, financial issues, and the list goes on. Many people hold those struggles inside all to themselves. If you can lead with compassion and understanding, even though you may not understand their actions or words, it could go a long way toward giving them some comfort as well as giving you some peace of your own. Some may be short-tempered or even withdrawn for no reason. Try not to take it personally and act the same way back to them. Instead, take a few minutes to pause and try to understand that there may be something so much bigger than you can see; then, offer kindness or words of compassion. That will go a long way for them.

God wants us to love others as he loves us. If you look into someone's eyes—and try to feel their soul and emotions—you can begin to open your heart and mind to their struggles instead of letting your mouth or actions take the lead. There are some people who have a bigger struggle than you can ever imagine that lives deep within them. Some people live in a dark and hurtful place and it is not your job to fix them. Yes, I understand it is difficult and painful to watch, but some go so deep that only professional help (and a personal decision to change) can turn them around. Offer direction if they are open to it and a silent prayer if they're not. Sometimes, it's the silent prayer that will do the greatest good for you when you feel helpless.

Always remember, we are made up of energy, so protect your energy with all you have. I know you understand what it means when people say that some people "suck the life out of you." It's a strange phrase, but it is sometimes true.

As Zig Ziglar says, "You can have everything in life you want, if you will just help other people get what they want." This is more than true. I have many times volunteered or stepped in to help someone else when I had very little free time, but I made time because I knew I had much to give. I was always glad I did and always felt like I got more out of it than they received. The giving will come back to you when you least expect it, and it will be ten-fold.

I always followed this motto in my sales career as well. If I took care of my customers and distributors, I was always more than taken care of in the end. Conducting myself in this way has led to a very successful career in sales. Always be on a mission to serve others—make it about them. People love to feel needed, wanted, taken care of, and special. Once you put this into practice, the law of attraction will bring it back to you. What you put out you receive back.

Helping others and giving of yourself feeds your soul and will make your life more abundant than you could imagine. There will be days when you just feel like you have nothing to give; it's those days you step back and remember that someone is always dealing with a bigger difficulty or larger hurdle than what you are facing. It will put your problems in perspective, and feelings of gratitude take over when you remember you have so much to be thankful for. This alone will put you back on your feet so you can continue on your path.

If ever you're having a bad day, please take a few hours or an afternoon and volunteer. Find something that interests you; whether it's the animal shelter, local food bank, or helping out at school, step out of your normal routine (or what you think is a bad day) and spend some time giving back. When you volunteer in your local community or on a mission trip, it will put the bad day you are having in perspective. You will see that it's not so bad. I understand that volunteering looks great on a resume or application, but do it because you want to, and you enjoy giving back. It will mean more to you in the low times. It will get your mind off yourself and your idea of bad circumstances, and it will redirect your focus onto others.

I am very proud to raise my girls in the Catholic faith. Some may not agree or understand our religion, but the Catholic

Church does a lot of good in this world. Be proud to support your church and its efforts. My girls watch me give every Sunday, and they learned at an early age that we value our church home and family. I tell my girls to give even when you have very little, because you can fully trust that God will provide for your needs. Somehow your needs will always be met, and you just may be that angel that someone needs when giving. I'm telling you because I've experienced it. As a single mom supporting two little girls, there have been times when I didn't have much in the bank. Despite my situation, I still tithed every week and somehow, some way, God always made sure what I needed was there and blessed us with so much more. I prayed many times that my many blessings would be a blessing to others.

My girls have gone with me to collect food for the food bank and have shopped at Thanksgiving picking up a meal for a family in need. They have picked angels off the Christmas tree at school, and they have gone shopping to select the "wished for" items and then some. We have packed toiletry bags together to hand out at stop lights to someone with a sign. We've picked out teddy bears for our priest, Father Dan, to ship to Jamaica, and when I watched the girls hand them over to him, the smiles on their faces were worth every penny. Remember those times and then create many more throughout your life, providing a selfless example and shining light to those around you. Remember, you are influencing your children and those around you every moment of your life. Be intentional about how you live and show others love; it's contagious, and many who are watching will step up to join you. When you wake each morning, be thankful for another day, and then always ask God, "How can I be of service today to you and those around me?" Grow into this practice and watch how God speaks to you. You will be amazed at the abundance you will feel, the opportunities to give of yourself that come up, and the "co-inky-dinks" that arise that will put you in the right place at the right time to give of yourself to others. This will impact your relationships, your career, your family, and the life you live. Do it and watch how giving—when it's not "about you"—really gives back to you more than you could ever imagine.

NO EXCUSES!

There is no excuse not to learn and grow constantly. Education, both formal and informal, is a must to keep you growing. Successful people are never content and are always looking for ways to grow.

Make yourself uncomfortable so that you are stretched, challenged, and taken to new heights–far from your comfort zone. You'd be surprised what you are capable of when you learn new things and surround yourself with the right people. Sometimes it's not what you are learning in the class, group, or meeting, but rather it's the connections you make with the people around you. If you're not putting yourself in situations where you want your life to be, you will not see what's possible and learn from those before you.

Find your strengths and grow them; they will take you places, and quite often, are tied to what you are most interested— possibly even passionate—about. But, always keep in mind, it's a good idea to know the basics in other areas as well; if you need more in-depth help in these areas, hire someone. I know a little about taxes and investing, but I have an accountant do my taxes. I have a financial advisor who helps with my retirement and kids' funds. I go to someone I trust to help with silver, gold, and coin collections. I may know a little or, at least, enough to ask some educated questions to ensure I'm going in the right direction, but even if I don't, I can be sure the information is on that the electronic device in my hands and is just a click away.

One word of caution when researching (sometimes ad nauseum) various topics: please, don't get caught up in the learning and never get to the doing. We can watch podcasts, IGTV, Lives, Groups, YouTube, etc., every day, but if we don't put what we've learned into action, we won't grow. It's the doing that will grow you more than just learning ever will. Sometimes, you just need to take the step to *do*, regardless of whether you know everything or not. If you wait for life to be perfect before you go and conquer what you are dreaming of, you may be waiting for quite a while because the timing is rarely ever perfect. A decision to try, fail, grow, and try again is what will get you much further in life and in the direction of your dreams.

College is important, but it's not everything. I would encourage you to at least continue your education until you complete some sort of degree or trade certification. It's important to finish even when it gets hard, when (you think) you've changed your mind, or you've stumbled into something that doesn't require a college degree. Once you stop or "take some time off," it's very hard to go back and get back in the groove again. Remember, you are never alone; there's always support if you'll just reach out. Single moms have gone back to school; new moms with babies in tow and people with two jobs fit it in because they know better opportunities will come out of it.

But I warn you not to make college a place where you lose yourself and stall–dragging it out because you haven't quite figured out what you want to do. Do we ever figure it out? I don't think so. I was fully set on being a child psychologist. Yep. That didn't happen. I switched majors and decided to move to Florida, gave up all of my scholarships—hopefully, you remember that lesson from an earlier chapter—and was set on being a physical therapist.

Well, let's say that didn't happen when I failed anatomy and had to drop the course because my rats died after a vasectomy and tubal ligation project. I was so upset. I knew I wasn't cut out to finish the required courses, so I went back to psychology with a minor in health services so I could still graduate on time. But what can you do with a bachelor's degree in psychology? Absolutely nothing. So, I went on to earn a master's degree.

Getting an MBA was the best decision I ever made. Not only do the letters look good after your name, but you gain so much knowledge in those business courses that help you in your career just as much as your own life. This is where I fell in love with finance and learning the stock market. I learned how to read and understand a P/L (Profit and Loss) statement and balance sheets. Learning these skills helped me not only in business, but also in my personal finances.

Finance classes will help you learn about investing, which will pay off later in life when you are looking for time freedom—time to do what you want, time to take a vacation, or having a little extra income to raise some little girls (wink, wink) without working extra hard because these investments will be paying you a passive income.

In my finance class, we did case studies of large companies. As part of the study, we learned to understand a SWOT (strengths, weaknesses, opportunities, and threats) analysis—an essential tool in business. I have found that it is also helpful to me personally when I am making just about any major life decision. Yep, the next time you are facing a big decision, sit down and do a grid of strengths, weaknesses, opportunities, and threats. It will show you a clear picture of decision making at its finest. So please, even if you don't major in business, take a few classes to help you manage your way through life.

I'll be honest, though, you will not learn everything in college. So many people put a value on having a college degree or getting a degree before they can start their adult life. But there are a lot of people out there creating the life they want or finding their passion who do not have a college degree. In some careers, a degree is not necessary. Heck, with the internet and entrepreneurism, a degree may never be necessary. Still, if possible, try to learn the basics in college because our public education system for K-12 is very broken. I hope to teach my girls many of the basics before they ever graduate high school.

And keep in mind, we all have this incredible device at our fingertips where we can learn anything we ever want in life in a few short clicks to an article, blog, video, or live feed. Life is a continuous lesson. Always have a good list of books, and I'm not talking about a novel—although it's nice to get lost in those—I'm talking about books that expand your mind. I remember sitting on a plane once and the gentleman sitting next to me asked if I was reading my book for a class. I told him no, I was just reading it as it seemed to be a good book. The look I got... but it made me realize how many people do not read books to expand their minds, teach them something, or facilitate growth. Oh, the book I was reading? *The Human Genome Project*, which is about genetics and DNA research.

Zig Ziglar's bestseller *See You at the Top* was one of the first sales books I ever read, and I can't even begin to tell you what an impact it had on my life, especially as I was heading into sales. I owe a great many closed sales and successes to Mr. Ziglar. Robert T. Kiyosaki's *Rich Dad Poor Dad* greatly influenced my finances and helped me overcome debt. Suze Ormond has written many books geared towards women and their finances. Tony Robbins is at the top of my list for motivation, determination, and achieving great things in life. Grant Cardone will get you pumped up and motivated with his 10x life philosophy. Gary Vee, as he's known on Instagram, will put you in your place, push you to forget failure, or encourage you to go find yourself and what excites you. He will also shut down any excuse you ever come up with for why you can't do something.

I constantly have a list of books, and when I come across a new one or one is recommended to me, it gets added to my never-ending list. Quite frankly, it doesn't matter how you take in content—whether it's a hardcover or paperback, audio, or digital book or even a podcast—consume content that will help you continue to grow. I also suggest attending seminars to fuel your passions, make connections, and energize you to do more.

To grow exponentially, you need not only accountability partners, but a coach. Think about it. Athletes hire specialized coaches to help their performance. Singers hire vocal coaches. There are financial coaches, health and wellness coaches, career coaches, and life coaches, just to name a few. If you are looking to stretch yourself, learn from an expert, and grow quickly, a coach will do wonders for you. Just this past year, I hired two coaches to help with my personal growth and with writing this book. I couldn't speak more highly of them. They stretched me to learn about myself and where I was lacking, and then to take steps to improve my life. They were by my side throughout writing this book. They believed in me, even when I didn't believe in myself. They helped me through when I wanted to give up or couldn't see the possibilities in myself. I learned so much from them this year, and those lessons will continue to give back to me and my life for many years to come.

I will say in learning, taking chances, growing, and stepping out of your comfort zone, there will be so many opportunities that will come your way. Remember that everything you say "yes" to in life and each item you add to your to-do list limits something else you could be doing. Choose your yeses wisely, otherwise, you could be forced to say no to something that would inspire you because you are simply stretched too thin.

Saying yes to learning and stepping into your greatness comes with difficult times. Not everything will be easy and flow your way. My advice: embrace the "suck." Use the hard stuff to fuel you. Pay attention and learn from what is difficult. We sometimes perceive difficulties as failure. Failure may be setting us back because we just aren't ready for that level of life yet. It's in the failures we grow the most. Think about it: you don't grow and learn in the easy times nearly as much as through the missteps. There are so many lessons in the hard stuff. These lessons in life will remain with you forever once you learn them. Sometimes it takes a few failures to really understand and learn the lesson. Sometimes you only have to be shown once, and the lesson is easily understood. When you look back at your life, you will probably see that a lot of life's lessons got you where you are today. Lessons learned in formal education and from your family and friends, lessons learned by experience, lessons from books, and lessons from your coaches will shape your life and take you to the next level.

Never be good with the routine life that is just getting by daily. Learning will not only help you, but it will also help others around you who will learn from you and take their life to the next level—and isn't that what life is all about?

"If you are not willing to learn, no one can help you.
If you are determined to learn, no one can stop you."
—*Zig Ziglar*

So, when you find yourself lying low in the status quo, what is the story you keep telling yourself? Find out what the root of it is. Heal it—and move on. Every day should bring growth, challenge, happiness, and learning. Your life should not look the same in five years or ten years when you look back; if it does, you are not living. You are lying low. Go do something you've always wanted to do; learn something you've always wanted to know. Learn to better your finances. Go learn about nutrition or the human body to better your health. Go learn about marketing to grow your business or learn skills to help you communicate better with your kids, spouse, coworkers, or employees. Go learn something new, build upon what you know, or learn something new. It's the small building blocks that lead to enormous growth when you look back in life. Be bold and tackle life.

ICE CREAM SMILES FOR DECADES TO COME

One day I took a drive to Virginia with my mom and girls to visit my Aunt Vickie. That afternoon we hung out at the restaurant she and my uncle opened together. The restaurant was packed with customers, all the servers were running around, and the kitchen was slammed. Despite the craziness, Aunt Vickie took the time to step away from it all to spend time with us. It was a beautiful day; the weather was perfect, and lots of visitors were walking the streets.

The girls wanted ice cream, so we all took the golf cart down to the ice cream stand. We sat on the picnic bench and ate our ice cream, talked, laughed, and hung out. We left the ice cream stand and headed over to the little coffee shop where I grabbed a coffee before heading back to the restaurant. I remember that Saturday like it was yesterday. That was April of 2016. The very next month, my Aunt Vickie would be diagnosed with brain cancer and would undergo emergency brain surgery—just two days after diagnosis.

Aunt Vickie spent months in the hospital going through chemo and radiation. When she was finally released, she was confined to a wheelchair. She was no longer be able to feed herself, dress herself, bathe herself, or fix her hair like she used to.

I have so many memories with my Aunt Vickie, but that afternoon having ice cream and just hanging out sticks with me the most. What if we hadn't decided to venture over to Virginia that day? What would my last fond memory of spending time together be? I mention this because it is always my gentle reminder to make time for the little things, because time is not promised. Tomorrow is not guaranteed to anyone.

I can certainly tell you "things" will not last, but experiences will. Travel, concerts, sharing with friends, day events, retreats, and just plain enjoying the moment—that's what lasts. I try so

49

hard to put this into perspective with my girls. I explain that the "things" they think they want right now are not worth nearly as much as if they were to put the money towards an experience. And even then, some experiences cost nothing or very little. A bag of worms from the tackle shop and grabbing the fishing poles makes for a quiet and relaxing day on the water with my girls to just catch up with each other. A bike ride through the neighborhood or playing with sidewalk chalk can bring many smiles.

There is nothing like taking my girls on adventures, and from an early age, they both have loved to travel with me. Many people say they can't afford to travel, and I always wonder *How can you afford not to?* To get away, relax, smile, and experience different activities makes life so memorable. It can be done on a budget and with a family. When you have a goal as a family to take a trip, have the discussion about what you want to do and what it will cost—I can assure you the family will be behind the saving part for the trip when they are looking forward to the fun and memories that will be made. My girls think of a plane as a "mechanical magic carpet" taking them to places to see and things to do. Their Christmas lists almost always have some sort of trip or experience on them in place of "stuff." They look forward to doing things as a family, laughing, and smiling. We talk about things we've done and places we've been. I think it's important to show them life outside of the small county we live in.

Life is short and can change in an instant. I learned this at a very young age. I still have flashbacks whenever I see a motorcycle accident. I was home just before Christmas break my freshman year of college, studying for finals. My parents had gone out with my uncle to have dinner and spend time together. A short time later, my uncle and mom pulled up at the house in my uncle's truck, but my dad, who was on his motorcycle, did not. So, they drove back the way he would have come and found Dad in the middle of the road, where a man was putting a tourniquet on his leg.

I was at the house, unaware of any of the drama that was unfolding just a few blocks away, until my mom called, crying hysterically. I jumped in my car and drove around to the accident in my boxers and tee shirt with my hair in a bun and my eyes tired from studying. It didn't stop those eyes from crying like never before. I fell to the cold street and let out a scream at the sight of my dad lying in the road in a pool of blood, the motorcycle on its side and the back end of a car smashed up where he had struck it. His leg had gotten stuck in the wheel well and was ripped off at the scene.

To this day, every time I see the man who had administered first aid—who happened to be a police officer—I thank him again for saving my dad's life. The accident happened right in front of the officer's house and if it hadn't been for his quick thinking, my dad would have not survived.

The scene was horrific. The paramedics were picking up tissue and pieces of his leg and putting it all into a bag to send in the helicopter with him in hopes that the surgeons at the hospital could piece him back together. At one point, they were going to call off the helicopter transport because Dad had lost six pints of blood and was in such critical condition, they didn't hold out much hope. But the man with the will to live was conscious enough to tell them he was still there, and they all continued to fight for him.

Against all odds, he survived. He even walked again when every doctor said he never would. He lived another twelve years after the accident and, yes, he even rode a motorcycle again. But that night changed our family forever. The next year was hard with him being in the hospital and Mom traveling back and forth every day. I took over his carpet business and kept jobs going to bring in income while he was recovering.

Looking back, I can see how that moment and the accident defined how I would live my life. At 18 years old, when everyone thinks they are going to live forever and are invincible, I learned that life can change in a second. I realized then the importance of trying to live your best life and living in the moment. You never know what tomorrow or even later today may bring. After my dad got better, I decided to transfer colleges to go see and live in a different place and explore life.

When I was in my twenties with nothing to hold me in one place, I wanted to see the world. I knew it would be much harder when I got older and had a family, so, I traveled quite a bit then. When I look back, I'm so glad I did. My only regret was that I didn't do much international travel. Still, I traveled so much I had Platinum Elite status—well over 250,000 airline miles—before the age of 25.

I wanted a job out of college that paid me to travel and see the country. It was a vision board item for me (more on that later!), and so it was that in my early twenties, I created this vision for what I wanted and within a few weeks of completing grad school, I landed my dream job. I have seen almost all 50 states on someone else's expense account. I traveled and set up trade show booths to sell microscopes and science supplies. My stops included Austin, with the bats under the bridge. I went to Boise, which is absolutely beautiful, and I shipped the biggest potatoes ever back home. San Antonio has the magnificent River Walk. Chicago is where I saw Oprah, and I visited Harley Davidson and toured a beer factory while in Milwaukee.

My life was a blur for a while because I was taking about 35 trips a year, but I loved it and wouldn't trade those days for anything. I often reflect on the experiences, places, and people I met along the way. I did some pretty cool things and saw some amazing sights. That work travel also gave me "points" to use personally for flights and hotels to destinations like Cabo San Lucas and Lake Tahoe, which to this day are still some of my favorite spots.

One thing I still need is a constant reminder of how to *make time*—even if only small blocks of time. We tend to get so busy and caught up in life, that we are not truly experiencing the blessings God has put in our lives. As the saying goes, we need to stop and smell the roses. The to-do list will never get completely done. Sometimes you have to put it to the side and live in the moment. Have fun, enjoy life, and do what you want today, because I promise you, the to-do list will always be there. As a matter of fact, if something happens to me, please bury that list with me because, at the end of the day, it will never get scratched off completely. You will always have something on your list and that is ok. But what is not ok is not taking time to enjoy this great life that's been given to you. Make the most of each day, and every now and then, look up from that electronic device to see the blessings put in your path each day. Experiences, not things, are so much more fulfilling, a lot more exciting to talk about, and will make you smile when sharing. Sometimes, it's the very little things like stopping your day to take 30 minutes to have ice cream on a bench in the middle of the afternoon that create smiles for decades to come.

"Doing nothing often leads to the very best of something."
—*Winnie the Pooh*

MASTERING YOUR MINDSET MATTERS

Words have power. Words can stick with you, repeat themselves, and become a force to be reckoned with. Words can create beliefs, and sometimes, those beliefs end up stuck in your head. Those beliefs carry with them consequences. If you had to choose, would you rather those consequences be good or bad? I'm pretty sure I know the answer. You would not intentionally choose bad, hurtful, negative, and harmful outcomes for yourself. So, I ask, why put those words into your head and allow them to shape your mind in ways that cause you to believe so little of yourself? Words are sometimes said to you in the most casual way, or maybe the words and beliefs are formed by your environment. Don't let the power of negative words run over you—it can take years to overcome the beliefs that get ingrained in your mind.

What is the story you keep telling yourself? If it's a negative one or one with limitations, find out where that story came from. I'm sure it came from words—words you heard or words you started to tell yourself. Find the root of that story so you can begin to heal where it came from and move on. For me, it was always wondering what people would think or say. I may say that I do not care what people think, but on the inside, we all crave acceptance, and we fear being put down. Like most people, we ask ourselves, "Who am I?" or, "Why me?" or, "Will they like it or me?" It isn't until later in life that we learn that most people do not give a crap. Most people are too busy dealing with their own issues, insecurities, beliefs, and words to care what you are doing. There will be those select people who do care, and if they are your people, they will root you on through all of your crazy ideas and wildest dreams.

I've been told at various times in my life that I intimidate people and come across as a b*tch. That's a pretty negative belief to hear, ingrain, and carry with you throughout life. It can be a limiting belief. Those who have gotten to know me will say that it's not true and complete crap, but I've carried it around, nonetheless. Would you carry a bag of trash with you everywhere you go? At some point, you have to take out the trash and let that negative energy go. I often wonder if, when hearing the words, at some point, I made them bigger than they needed to be. It took me years of self-discovery to realize it was something I was telling myself and most people didn't actually see that in me. What are you telling yourself? Is it something you heard? I can say from experience, if it's negative and sticks in your head, it is not God talking. You wouldn't want to hang out with people who talk to you in a negative way, so stop talking to yourself that way. God gave you your story for a reason. Once you own your story, accept it, and use it, you will be a game changer.

So many people are dealing with their own struggles. Some will say things to you based on their belief system and how they feel about themselves. Like those who say "Wow, must be nice," when commenting on something you do or have. Or "You shouldn't do that," when you live outside the boundaries that they've set for themselves. Or, "That's not normal," when you do something that makes them uncomfortable. Well, who defines normal? Who says you shouldn't do something you want to do? Who says you should live small and not do big things? If you can learn to listen to others with a heart to understand where they're coming from instead of simply getting your feelings hurt and internalizing their comments, you will save yourself years of pain.

There are those people in the world whom you shouldn't allow in your life for the long term, but sometimes they pass through your life only for the lesson or blessing they were meant to be and move on. I have been in one too many verbally abusive relationships in my past. Looking back, it would have been easier for me if I had been physically abused than for me to hear and ingrain those words into my belief system. You choose how people treat you and you decide what you are willing to listen to. Be careful, because those words you are hearing will be what you start telling yourself. What you tell yourself and repeat in your mind tends to show up more in your life. As Aunt Vickie would say, you can manifest your life by what you believe and tell yourself daily. Not everyone is here for the same purpose, life, and path. Also, remember that sometimes it's not about you; it may have been for *them* that your paths crossed. They may just need someone to listen and understand their pain in that moment.

Think of letting go of a negative mindset and those harsh words we tell ourselves as LENT. Lent is a time of rebirth. Sometimes we need to sit alone in quiet and learn to listen to ourselves and what we are saying internally. LENT–Let's End Negative Thoughts. Dig deep to find the root and cut it off there. I tell my girls all the time that "can't" is not a word in our house. I have always seen *can't* as a negative word. Like so many motivated people, you tell me that I can't do something; but, I will do it twice and take pictures along the way. *Can't* is a limiting belief. Why would you want to limit the life that God has given you? There are no limits to the life you can live, the things you can do, the places you can see, the people you can touch. I dare you to create and dream the biggest and boldest life possible. If we all just learned to not care what others' opinions are, I think we would all pursue our real dreams a whole lot more. The big dreams scare us, and the doubters make us question our ability. It's time to surround yourself with supporters and step up into that big life you've dreamed of having. It's your life. You've got one life, so go live it!

As long as I'm here, I will support and encourage those looking to pursue their dreams. What a life well lived, when we can look back with no regrets to see the life we created. Negative words and mindsets impose limits on us. How do you show up for yourself when no one is looking (to judge you)? That's how you should show up for yourself daily, because I'm sure you are not fearful and limiting when no one is watching and offering their opinions. Do you find yourself singing in the car or dancing in the house while doing chores? How about creating projects you never share, like artwork or writing? I dare you to just do it at any given moment, regardless of who's watching or reading. Decide what you want in life with no limits and negative self-talk. Lead by example and you may be surprised that you fall in love with who you are. Change that Belief System from Bull Sh*t to Big Soul. Be that person who is a light to yourself and others with words that raise up instead of tearing down.

Manifesting was explained to me by my Aunt Vickie. What you focus on tends to show up more in your life. The universe has a way of showing up for you. What you put in your mind comes out daily around you. If you pay attention, you may be surprised. Negative thoughts and energy bring about a bad day and more negativity. If you look at everything as a blessing in your life and find the little blessing in what was supposed to be a negative situation, the day is not ruined, and you are able to move on much quicker.

Zig Ziglar used to say, "Failure is an event, not a person." If you failed, you are not a failure, it's just a moment in time. If you choose hurtful words to tell yourself when you fail, you will never learn and heal from the failure. You learn and grow from mistakes, so find the blessing and move on. Do not keep that failure and negativity in your head and put it on "repeat" daily.

Wake up each day with the promise and optimism of what you get to accomplish that day; follow the small steps that will lead you to your big dreams. Manifest and create the life you want by learning to build yourself up, and you will see life show up for you. You will attract and bring about what you deserve and are willing to accept. Don't ever accept less than you know you deserve. Own yourself. Own your thoughts. Own those words in your mind—they will shape your days, weeks, months, and years ahead. "You can do anything you put your mind to," as my momma would always tell me. Anything. Be open to possibilities. Say yes to everything that excites you deep inside. Say yes to opportunities that will push you out of your comfort zone and help you grow. Say yes to life experiences that create joy and happiness.

There is no room for negative thoughts and fear. You may suck at some things, but that's okay. You're going to be seen taking the risk, opportunity, or challenge and stepping up in life. You will be remembered for that and not for the missteps you took or not being perfect. Many older people at the end of their life regret what they should have done, or what they wish they had done. Well, why didn't they? Was it the thoughts in their mind that prevented them? The can'ts or shouldn'ts of other people's opinions got in the way. When it's the voices around you that are stopping you or pulling you down, you need to walk away. Walk away from where you've been to get to the place you need to be. Change your surroundings if you need to. Change the people you spend time with. Most importantly, learn to change your mindset in a matter of minutes. Stop yourself when those negative words creep in and give yourself five affirmations: You are capable. You are beautiful. You are smart. You are courageous. You are strong.

Always change for the better, or at least take a path to get moving in that direction and away from negativity. It may not always be "the" path, but it's "a" path toward something better than the gloom a bad mindset brings. Manifest and create the life you want in your mind, tell the universe, and watch the co-inky-dinks show up. Take massive action often towards your dreams and you will start to see your dreams can become reality. Who or what is stopping you? I hope it is not the words and stories you are telling yourself. No action is not an option; it's today or never. If you progress toward those dreams, I promise life will bring you happiness. Happiness is not about stuff or what you have; it's about fulfilling your deepest dreams and desires in life. What do you want your life to look like? Now, go running in that direction as if you were on fire, because life is too short not to. Show others what is possible and show up for yourself.

God has a plan. Know when you follow him, you are always on the verge of something great when you least expect it. If you can believe something special is always just around the corner, or that you are just one person away from an encounter that could be the network you need, you will quickly learn how a change of feeling and belief in your mind can change your destiny. If you look at a door closing as a loss or defeat, you will feel and tell yourself that you've suffered a defeat. But what if you look at a door closing as an opportunity to go another direction, to say yes to something bigger that you would have missed if you had gone through that first door? A "no" should not be looked at as a negative, but more of a "yes" in another direction.

What makes you change a negative thought to a positive in that moment is a result of how you have trained your mind to see things in life. Make sure it's the positive and not negative. Find the lessons in the failures and always speak to yourself with kind words. Don't tell yourself those negative thoughts and dumb yourself down. It only limits you and your life. Negative thoughts create a small life, and God did not put you here for that. Don't play small and have a small quality of life. Learn to raise your standards and change your own thoughts and those you hear from others to thoughts that will build you up. You will live emotionally wherever your mind is. Repeat that. Again. Small minds—negative minds—create anxiety, depression, and a life of feeling beat-down daily. Build your mind, change your outlook, and make your life bigger than you could ever imagine. Turn "I can't" into "I did" and "I should" into "I must". No one is watching like you think they are, so drop that idea because it will hold you back. Find the freedom that comes from mastering your mind and see what is possible in life. I know for sure that what is in your mind will show up—why not make it unbelievable? Go manifest the heck out of your life so that one day you can look back and say, "Wow, what a ride!"

BE VISION DRIVEN AND GOAL FOCUSED

I had an interesting conversation with someone the other day. It was someone I would consider to be pretty successful, someone who manages and mentors many employees under them. But he seemed uneasy and lacked energy. My question to him, "Do you have a written vision statement of where you want your business to go so that the employees will know what they are a part of?" The answer was "No." I was shocked. His business is growing, but it could be so much more if everyone knew the direction and vision. What if he woke up every day with a clear intention and goal for his company? What if he had a vision statement? What if we all had a vision statement for our lives?

A vision statement expresses where you are headed, but not what the plan is to get there. That's where goals come in. I was going through some papers the other day and stumbled on my goals from when I moved back to Maryland. They covered the years 2001-2005. I had taken a break from goal setting right after my dad died in 2005, which was followed by my marriage in 2007 and crazy baby life in 2008, up until my separation.

I started writing my goals down again just a couple of years ago. Life was dramatically different when I was setting goals, having something to look forward to, and not living each day on repeat. You will regret the years that you sat back and didn't write your goals in order to help you pursue your dreams; I know I do. I wonder what I could have accomplished, checked off my bucket list, visited, or created.

Today, I write my goals based on the different areas in my life; because remember, what you focus on expands. For me and many others, it's nice to try and have a balanced life to look at areas where you may be lacking or need to focus to get your crap together. You can look up setting goals using the wheel of life, which will give ideas for what areas are important to you.

What does your "pie of life" look like? Is it segments of financial, spiritual, physical, relationships, learning, career, and family? You can choose what areas need work and make it unique for you.

It's understandable when you focus on some areas, others will fall short. We are all guilty of working on one problem area in our life and slacking off in others. But when you set goals in all areas, you tend to not neglect important parts of your life, because you are looking at your goals daily, and each area may have something you are working towards. What if you focused on work and career so much that you look up when you're 40 and realize that you are single and alone? If you only focus on money, but neglect the personal aspect, you'll end up with a pretty lonely life, wouldn't you agree? Don't get too busy making a living that you forget to design your life. Focus on where you want to go and have a clear, big, and bold vision.

A life well designed and lived purposefully is bound to make you look back and smile. Live with intention, dig deep, and find what makes you feel fulfilled. What invokes that inner child and makes you smile? What can you do for hours and get so engrossed in that you lose track of time? Make sure some of those things are on your list of goals. When life gets busy and the responsibilities of family, home, and career kick in, it's usually those passions and hobbies that get pushed to the side. Ask any working mom of young kids and you will usually hear that they feel they lost themselves among the sleepless nights, piles of clothes, dishes, field sidelines, and late-night homework help.

Most of us have experienced times when we look back and wonder where the time has gone and what have we actually done that was really important? As a Type A, I had to quickly learn to let things go. The laundry can wait a day, the floors can wait a day, the dishes can be done later, but the things that lead to checking off the bigger boxes need to get done. If we keep filling our days up with the "little to-dos" that we all have to get done, we never get to the big stuff that is life changing! And that, my dear, is what makes magic!

I dare you to keep a list of your accomplishments. Journaling can be a great tool. It can help you keep track of the little steps you need to take and took to get to the finish line, and it can help you look back at your accomplishments. If you can keep a running list of the big magic you made happen and the goals you had set that you never thought you could achieve, you will be able to show yourself what you've been able to do. At those times when you are being hard on yourself, this list will show you what you are capable of and remind you of things you accomplished that you hadn't thought possible. It will show you there are so many more and bigger things God has planned for you and your life if you keep at it. If you keep your goals and dreams written down, it's hard to lose sight of where you want to go in life. Know what you want and why you want it, but focus on the second half–the why.

> *"Success is getting what you want.*
> *Happiness is wanting what you get."*
> *–Dale Carnegie*

The success of checking off the goal is not as important as the person you become and the happiness you find while tackling the goal. It's not about reaching the end goal (because often times we will look at it and say, "Is that all there is?"), but rather it's about who you become while chasing the goal. If you have a goal of being financially successful, that's great, but what comes about from you being financially successful? The opportunities you provide others if you are a business owner can bring financial wellbeing to your employees' lives. Giving back and supporting youth teams or a charity is done more easily when you have been blessed with expanded finances. What did you learn from getting fit and losing 20 pounds? How can you use that to help others and be the one to show what is possible? Strong moms raise up their daughters and other women using lessons they've learned from their personal struggles to show them what is possible. Learn to show not just the highlight reel, but the baby steps it took to get you there, because only then can others learn from your mistakes and avoid the pitfalls.

People who write on this topic will tell you, you are more likely to achieve your goals if you write them down. Written goals give you something to look at daily. Written goals give you a statement to break down into a plan of action. If you follow through on enough actions, nothing can stop a goal from being realized. Written goals, when broken down, do not seem so overwhelming to conquer. I tell you from experience, I have had more growth in all areas of my life when I have clearly written goals.

The question is: where do you start? Do you have a "Power Hour" as some call it? If you don't have an hour, how about you "Thrive in Thirty"? You are only as busy as you tell yourself. Decide today to take a few Mindful Minutes that can help you to focus and plan for the day ahead as well as reflect as it winds down. Choose your priorities well, because you will always find time for what you prioritize and what's important to you. A mom will find time to get it all in for their children, but aren't you also a priority? Plan to work your day with intention towards your goals and dreams. What three things are important today to get you closer to checking off that bigger goal? Do you take time to start your day looking forward to opportunities, deciding what needs to get tackled, and pausing to look around to be grateful for another day given to make it happen? Life is better when you are passionate about your life and what makes up your day.

Being normal and living the same day will get you average. Average anything will not get you to an extraordinary life. You need to set goals and take massive action to get big results. What goal would you set that you could become obsessed with? What would your life look like if you went after a dream to make it a reality? What if that dream was so big you needed God to intervene to make it happen? Sometimes it's that voice inside that is God speaking to you to guide you. He believes in you and what you are capable of; now it's your turn to prove it to yourself.

It's amazing to look back at my goal lists over the years. What I once thought of a big goal makes me chuckle now. You see, when you start to tackle goals that you have written down in areas of your life and focus on them, your life expands in those areas. What was once a big goal, seems small looking back because you are now at a higher level. Then you add on to that goal or take it up a notch. You don't see the building blocks while you are climbing them, but the view from the top looking back will amaze you.

It's time to level up. It's time to raise your standards and value yourself because you are worth it. If you don't feel worthy, you may want to take a look at how your goal setting has been influenced by your upbringing. Are you able to think big enough? Do you "dumb down" your goals so you are "normal" and ordinary? People can only support your dreams and visions as far as they can see them. I want you to squeeze every drop of your desires out of your lifetime. If it were easy, everyone would be doing it. It's time to get clear and create a bigger vision. You can't see the future and design your life if you are focusing on the past. Remember, failure is an *event,* not a person. Do not focus on where you've been but on where you want to go, what you want to do, and who you want to become. Start today to go as far as you can see toward your goals; and then you will begin to see further once you know what is possible. God has bigger plans for you than you could ever dream or envision.

If writing goals is important, where do those goals come from? Visualize and imagine your dreams in great detail, put them in writing using the present tense as if those dreams were already a reality. Grab pictures to create a vision board so you have it mapped out, showing exactly what you want and what you are looking for. I promise you, the more vivid and realistic, the more likely it is that it will come true in your life.

Aunt Vickie taught me to visualize my life inside my head and then transform it onto paper, pictures, and words to make them come to life. She taught me about vision boards, dream boards, affirmation statements, and manifesting life. I think of them as some of my Vickie-isms. It's like she's smiling and winking at me from above when I start to daydream to manifest my life. I believe our loved ones come back to visit. They look over and watch us through our successes and failures. They smile and celebrate when we achieve our goals. I know when I'm no longer a physical being on this earth, my spirit will visit often to surround my girls on their brightest days and be the light in their darkest hours. I want to know when I can no longer be by their side, offer advice, and give help—they will always remember the lessons I taught them the way my Aunt Vickie taught me. She taught me to dream the biggest dreams for my life, and that's what I want for you. Dream big, my dear, and go manifest the sh*t out of life.

How often do you sit and daydream? I used to think of daydreaming as a waste of time, and that I could be doing other more "productive" things. But science and studies show the need for us all to slow down and find some quiet and stillness in our day. Our world is so busy and loud that we no longer have much time or a place to be still so we can dream and imagine the life we were created to live.

What dream would you want to make a reality? What goal would you set if you knew you could achieve it? Dreaming big for your life takes the invisible and starts to make it visible. How do you take ideas, thoughts, and desires and make them a physical reality? Goal setting will get you there. Once you set your goals, it's determination and persistence that will see you through.

God gives us grace and faith; use your grit to get through the hard stuff. Everything is possible when you have an unrelenting will to achieve it. Desire will have you see it, but faith will get you through it. When you are struggling to reach the goals, and you feel there's no possible way to realize your dreams, it's time to reach up. Reach out to those strong women who have gone before you on the path. Just as it's great to accomplish goals and focus on your dreams, it's always important to encourage others on their path and there will be those who will encourage you and push you along yours. There will always be helpers along the way to give insight and open doors that you might not be capable of opening. No one is going to do it all for you; it's ultimately up to you, but know you are not alone. I've reached out to my mom and Aunt Vickie more than you can imagine for insight and guidance.

I am a firm believer in networking because it is usually not *what* you know but *who* you know. People will be happy to connect you to the right person if you just ask. Trust that when you put your desires and goals out into the universe the path will open up and lead you to the right people and places at just the right time. It's only you who will ever accomplish the things you want out of life. If you aren't getting what you want out of life, then you need to take accountability for your actions. Typically, it's not that the goal has changed, it's that you haven't done anything about reaching it. Don't wait around for things to happen, instead, take action and create the life you were created to live. It's not that you don't have the time to accomplish what you want out of life, it's that you are not focusing on the right things. When you say to yourself, *I just don't have the time,* I want you to hear God yelling back, "You don't get more time in a day, you need to give more of you!"

When you are pursuing your dreams, desires, and passions, focusing on the plan and accomplishing goals will give you the momentum to set your life on fire. That burning desire and the energy it creates will attract what's needed to make that vision a reality in your life. It's time to start dreaming big and manifesting the life you were created to live. As Mary Poppins says, "Everything is possible, even the impossible. Today or never—that's my motto."

HAPPINESS BEGINS WITH A WINK AND A SMILE - "CO-INKY-DINKS"

"Coincidence is God's Way of Remaining Anonymous"

—*Einstein*

When you learn to create and manifest the life you want, it will become apparent that your vibration level brings about events that make you pause and wonder how it all happened. Life will begin to happen in just the right ways when you remain in a positive state of mind and harness the power that mindset will provide you. Synchronicities will begin to take place that will make you smile when you look back at how it all unfolded. As Aunt Vickie would say, there are no coincidences. You will realize there is a higher power helping you along the way. If you pay attention to the signs around you, you will begin to see "winks" from the universe. Know that God always has perfect timing. You may want things to happen sooner, but when you are on the right path, in sync with your life plan, working to manifest the life you have imagined, and working hard towards your goals, you will begin to see the co-inky-dinks unfold before your eyes. Everything happens for a reason.

Not too long ago this was my realization. As I looked up from my laptop for a few minutes to reflect on my long day, I thought back to how I ended up where I am. The past few months have been a blur, just as looking at the computer screen has become a blur lately. Long days and nights of staring at a computer screen have resulted in me breaking down and ordering blue light glasses to help ease the eye strain. As I snap a picture to see what I look like with glasses on, I can't help but peer in the background at the Corona chair sitting in my office and chuckle. I chuckle at the thought of Aunt Vickie smiling down on me and seeing her chair in my office. I chuckle at the thought of the word "Corona" during the Coronavirus lockdown, and I chuckle at how much my life has evolved in just the last twelve months.

When you step into the possibilities, open up to what life has to offer, and let go of your agenda, you may be surprised at the path God takes you down–a path better than what you imagined or ever thought it could be. Sometimes the hard steps are the ones you need to take to grow, create the life you've imagined, and give the universe a chance to show up to make synchronistic magic happen.

Just over a year ago, I took an incredible leap of faith and moved my family into a new home. I was scared. Quite honestly, I was questioning what I was doing. I had built the home we were living in; it was comfortable, and it was the only home my girls had known all of their young lives. It was safe and easy, and it was our normal, but I knew I wanted more. I wanted a neighborhood where my girls would have friends, we could walk our dogs, ride bikes, and they could take the bus to school. I wanted a large yard where the dogs could run and where the girls could play outside without worrying about a car coming down the street. I wanted to start our family life over in a new house for us, making new memories. I wanted not just a house; I wanted a home.

I had been looking at houses for quite some time. I was hoping to find one that, from the moment I saw it, I would know it was home. I wanted to be on the water. We had been living just off the Chesapeake Bay for several years, and I didn't want to give up the calmness that being near water provides. I wanted to be in a certain area of our county so the girls could stay at the school they had been attending. I also selfishly wanted them to go to the same high school I had graduated from. Checking off everything on my wish list was not an easy feat.

I searched online—I'm sure, drove my Realtor crazy—and looked on and off for a few years. I remember attending adoration at church on the Friday night before I was to see a few houses with my Realtor. While praying, my conversation with God went something like this: "God. I just do not have it in me to build a house right now. My life is crazy. I can certainly build our dream home on my lot, but I don't think I could live through it without having a breakdown. Please, I beg you, tomorrow, would you guide me to the house I've been looking for? I am leaving it up to you to make this happen, because you know I cannot handle building right now, we are ready for a new home, and it's time to start a new chapter in our lives. I am letting go, God, and leaving it up to you—for your will to be done." I let go of my "house worry" that night and opened up to what was to come, knowing we were more than ready for a new chapter in our lives.

The next day, I looked at several houses. I ended up liking one and planned to revisit it the following week with my mom and girls so they could take a look. There was a house around the corner in the same neighborhood that was for sale. I can remember driving by and seeing that, as a matter of fact, it was on the water. I called my Realtor and asked if I could take a look at it, but she told me it was under contract. I asked again, "Just let me *look* at it so I can see what else is selling." She relented and made an appointment. After looking at the first house I'd seen, we waited in the car for our appointment time to visit the one under contract. When it was time, we made our way up the long driveway and heard the rippling sound as our tires rolled over the pavers. Just then from the backseat, Dani (my younger daughter) asked, "Are we at a hotel?" I giggled, because I realized that is what some hotel entrances sound like. When I had stopped the car, my Realtor came to my door to remind me that we were "just looking" because "the house is under contract." I just nodded and got everyone out of the car. The Realtor smiled and told us once more, before we entered the house, "Do not get attached."

We went in the double front doors, and I knew from the moment I stepped in, this place felt like home. The entrance reminded me of my great grandfather's house with that warm, cozy feel. We walked around to the family room where glass windows overlooked a stunning view of the river. Exactly what I wanted. The paint colors in the kitchen were the same as the house we were in, and it had a Viking gas stove, which was also on my checklist. The large laundry room and two-car garage off the kitchen rated yet another check. The master bedroom had the same colors as my bedroom, which meant my bedroom set, pictures, and furniture would match perfectly–as if it had been made for me to just move my belongings in. The office off the master bedroom—you guessed it—matched my current office.

When we finished our tour of the home, every single box was checked and then some. This house had everything that was on my list! Plus, it even had a built-in intercom system like the one I played with as a kid at my great grandad's house. We left that day, and I prayed about what to do. When you open up to the possibilities, life gives you more than you expect. I asked my Realtor to submit a back-up offer. As a matter of fact, I had to ask more than once, because my Realtor didn't want to do it, for fear I would lose out on the house around the corner. I told her, "If it's meant to be, it will be. If I lose out on the other house, then I wasn't supposed to have it," but I had a feeling this was my house. I felt that little nudge inside as if someone was telling me, "Just step out and take the chance." Let me show you what happens when you have faith enough to let go and let God.

Well as I sit in my office at that very house, I'm happy and proud to call it "home." The girls couldn't be happier. They tell me all the time that while they do miss our old house sometimes— since that was where they grew up—our home now feels like we've always lived here. The dogs love it here. They love to run, play, and chase all of the crazy animals on the land that surrounds our home. I feel blessed beyond belief. Did it scare me? Absolutely. It was a huge step for me. The house is a lot for a single mom and her family to take care of and maintain, but I wouldn't change it for the world. The sunset each night out back reminds me to slow down, reflect, and give thanks for the many blessings in my life. The setting sun calms me and reminds me that God is with me through the struggles. He will lead me down the path he has planned if I just allow him. He has more planned for us than we can imagine ourselves.

Have faith when you need something; God will provide. Have faith that God will bring along the right opportunities that are part of his plan. Open up to knowing that he is there for you every step of the way. Remember that it's not in *your* timing, but in *his* timing that God will show up. I'm positive that Einstein was on to something when he said, "Coincidence is God's way of remaining anonymous." He will send you a wink and a smile from above; call them *God Winks*, or as Aunt Vickie would say, co-inky-dinks. Learn to open your eyes and pay attention as they come in all forms.

It's not always just about the big events that line up or the unexplainable changes that impact your life so vastly you can't help but notice. Try paying attention to the little signs from above. When you are walking, and "just happen" to glance down at the right time to see a penny—that can bring a smile to your face if you are aware and allow it.

Signs can even come in the form of an animal. Aunt Vickie used to tell me to pay attention to the strange animals that cross my path. That cardinal that visits, or the hummingbird that buzzes by—because they are sometimes more than you think. You can easily look up the spirit meaning of an animal and find there may be a meaning behind their presence. What you will see once you start to become aware of your surroundings may just surprise you.

Numbers will also show up as co-inky-dinks. Seeing repetitive numbers can be a form of synchronicity as numbers have meaning and symbolism. Again, it may just surprise you once you start to become aware of your surroundings. You will begin to notice the God Winks that show up if you lead with an open mind and learn to pay attention. Always have faith, trust in his timing, and be on the lookout for the signs that tell you you're on the right path. Life is amazingly abundant and there for you when you need it most. God is watching and sending you signs that create a meaningful connection—a co-inky-dink.

THAT LITTLE VOICE
INSIDE YOU

There's a little voice inside you—listen to it. Aunt Vickie would always remind me to listen to my intuition as it always knows best. The Bible tells us to "Be still and know that I am God" (Psalm 46:10, KJV). Learn to be quiet and still so you can listen to his voice. Remember to hold fast to an hour or 30 minutes to dream during your day. Take additional time to sit in silence, pray, and form a relationship with God. He wants to guide you and get to know you deeply. We can call that voice God, spirit guides, intuition, gut feelings, female instinct—whatever name you want to give it, but I'm sure we can all say we've experienced it. If I had listened to that voice almost 15 years ago, I could have avoided many of the mistakes I made over those years. Some of those mistakes I'm grateful for, as I would not have my two girls had I not made them. I learned lessons the hard way and I'm better for knowing how to deal with some of life's challenges. God redeemed—or is still redeeming—the missteps of my past, but he and I both would've preferred it if I had done things his way in the first place. I'm learning to follow him much better. But how do you know it's him?

At first, the voice starts out small. It's that quiet voice that causes you to turn around thinking someone has just said something to you. You brush it off. Then the voice gets louder, but you continue to disregard it. Still, the voice gets louder, as it tries to tell you that your life is totally off-track. You find yourself one day sitting with your life as a total wreck, everything is upside down, and you feel totally unhappy. You're crying and wondering, *how did I get here?*

It's called "free will," my dear—*free will.* You didn't listen to that voice, and now you are on a totally different path than was meant for your life. It can be a very hard lesson to learn. And sometimes, if you don't learn it, you will be tested again and again.

Again, you'll hear the voice, like little nudges or questions. You will have worked so hard on picking yourself up from failure, putting your life back on the right path, and working on you, that hopefully the voice only has to speak once.

Sometimes we may hear the voice and actually get into an argument with it—try to avoid doing this aloud if you're in public...people tend to stare. In your head, you'll be trying to reason—or rationalize—with the voice about how *this time is different* or *I know what I'm doing*. When you have finished giving your best argument, remind yourself to listen to that voice; it knows best, and it's always right.

So, with that said, can you imagine what your life would be like if you learned to listen to that small voice? I'm sure many of you would have quit jobs, started a new career, moved, traveled, learned a hobby, followed a passion, chosen a different relationship, or not started certain relationships in the first place. Sometimes people even hear the voice telling them to give to the homeless man on the corner or talk to a stranger, and when they listen to it, they end up impacting a life in ways they never could've imagined. Some hear the voice when they pick up that bottle of alcohol after they have vowed to stop drinking. Or when you're trying to quit smoking, and, again, you try to reason with the small voice, explaining that "It's just one." The voice is addressing the addictions we need to overcome; it's reminding us of the life lessons that are continually digging at us.

The voice is there for a reason, but instead of listening, we sometimes ignore it because we think we know best—and using our free will—we choose against the advice of the voice. Sometimes we listen and change paths before the voice has to get too loud, but sometimes we need it to yell at us. I like to think of the voice as God speaking to me, and the times he is forced to yell at me are usually when I have stopped looking for him and listening to him. He was with me the whole time, watching me suffer unnecessarily because I was more interested in my own free will than paying attention to his plan for my life. You need to trust God with the results, but you must do your part by listening to his guidance.

When you wake up in the middle of the night and can't get back to sleep, that's God's wake-up call. You see, life is so noisy, and we are so busy that we don't take the time to slow down to rest, meditate, relax, sit still, and just *be*. Life is deafening at times. As moms, we are constantly running ourselves ragged for everyone else, managing not just our own schedule but our kids' schedules too. If you don't have children, but are married, you might be the one who manages the chores around the house, plans the vacations, and a lot of everything else. If you are single, you can get so busy filing your days with work, social activities, or nieces and nephews, that you leave yourself very little time to relax. Let's face it, life is mostly run at medium to high pace with very little time to slow down. Downtime is necessary if you're going to be able to hear and listen to that little voice. God wants to speak to you and develop a relationship with you. He can't seem to get through during our busy days, so he wakes us up at night in order to have a conversation. God's wake-up calls are his invitation to you to ask questions of him, seek his guidance, and give gratitude for his many blessings. God loves you, and he wants to be your divine parent. It is not only ok for you to seek him out for direction when you are struggling and lost on that path, it's imperative.

You can't run ahead of the Lord and rush the results—remember, it's in his timing anyway. Learn to have faith that everything will happen according to his plan, and while there may be plenty of things you don't understand, one day you will look back and be able to see the "why" behind it all. It's a struggle to tell yourself that, I know. But know that God has your back and only gives you what you can handle. He will give you the strength and grace to get you through it.

When things get hard, ask yourself *What am I grateful for?* If you will look at all of the graces and blessings he has given you, it will put the hard stuff into perspective. When you live with gratitude, you remember what got you where you are, and you can look at how far you have come. The hard stuff will not seem as hard when you have your eyes on the blessings and are thankful for them. Learn to stay grounded in grace and gratitude throughout life. Keep God in your heart and remain grateful for all that he has given you. Chase your goals with grit and determination. Let God radically transform your life as you listen to that inner voice the *first* time.

YOU HAD ME AT HELLO...

It's in your failures you find your greatest strength… but if you can remember one quote from Zig Ziglar, it will help you understand that you are *not* your failures, your failures are just events that happen. Learn the lessons from the failures, remember whose daughter you are, straighten your crown, and grow from the lessons they taught you.

The other day I was thinking about my past experiences and the lessons I've learned in the realm of relationships. It was then I realized this is the area of my life that I struggle with the most. If you were to look at most other aspects of my life, you'd be likely to think I have it all together. I am very driven, focused, and goal-oriented. I excelled throughout school. My health has, for the most part, always been good. I've been blessed to have a career that allows me to earn a decent living. My life seems to be great from the outside looking in. I've been told countless times that I have my sh*t together. I've been told by some that I seemed "perfect" or "not normal" until they have gotten to truly know me and have seen that I have struggles like everyone else. Many women you see may seem this way and it is even exacerbated by social media as everyone looks to have it all together. From the filters, success stories, and highlight reels, many appear perfect, and the viewer compares their life, feels less, and wonders how they do it. The reality is, we are all working on ourselves, and we all have struggles. What we should do as women is learn from the struggles of others just as much as the successes.

The one area in my life where I struggle the most is in relationships with men. Most people who know me would be shocked to know what I've tolerated in life. They would not understand how the strong woman and mother they think they know has been in more than one toxic relationship. I say this because many women, like me, are good at hiding the shame of putting up with ill treatment. Many women are good at holding it together in all other aspects of their lives, so you would never guess that things are very different behind closed doors. Many of the toxic relationships were with men whose behavior in private was not what others saw in public.

Our most important relational patterns are formed in childhood. The relationships you observe as you are growing up are what you perceive as normal. The lack of attention from a father can lead to unhealthy relationships later in life. Let's be clear: my parents never divorced. They were married until the day my dad died, but the relationship I witnessed was far from what a healthy marriage should look like. My dad cheated on my mom. My dad did drugs. My dad would go out drinking and partying at night, leaving my mom home with me. Don't get me wrong, he was a good dad, and I loved being his little girl, but he did not show me what a good *husband* looks like until much later in life when he began to demonstrate his love for my mother. But before that transformation, I witnessed verbal and physical abuse between them. I can remember my dad throwing dishes out the back door when my mom asked for his help. For my dad to call my mother a b*tch was not out of the ordinary. He used similar language toward me—although, he would play it off as a joke—I can remember him calling me a "little b*tch." My dad was not around too often as I grew up, which left my mom and me as a pair when it came to my activities, sports, and school. My mom basically raised me alone and showed me how a strong mom can make it through life.

While my mom's attention helped make me strong, my dad's *lack* of attention left me craving the love and attention of a man as I got older. The problem is, when you grow up watching an unhealthy relationship, you think that is the norm and you end up making bad relational choices and putting the "It's okay" label on it.

Abuse can come in many forms—verbal, physical, financial, and emotional. You should know that he doesn't necessarily have to hit you for it to be abuse. So many have experienced abuse in some way or another. I'm no different. I've been there. I've dealt with it. More than once. You'd be surprised how many women are in the same situation in which I found myself, but they conceal it out of humiliation. Once out of the relationship they may be fooling the rest of the world that all is well, but there are things that trigger those memories. That pain never fully goes away. It leaves scars that we live with, but we don't have to let those scars affect our future.

One of the hardest lessons in life is that some people will only ever think of themselves. The hurt you feel because of their actions doesn't affect them one bit, so figure out a way to let go and let God handle it. What we all need to do is to be still, be quiet, and listen. You'd be surprised how you can begin to feel another person's pain and sorrow if you take the time. So many people need someone to just listen and have compassion.

Some of us have been conditioned not to trust other people from our past experiences. We have been conditioned to not believe and to think things will always be the same. We are conditioned to shut down, to be hardened. We put up a wall that blocks out the bad we are trying to protect ourselves from, but that wall can also prevent love from coming into our lives. Don't have that wall. Take down the blocks and allow life and romance in.

Ask yourself in every relationship you may have, "Am I living? Am I loving?" We would have much different relationships if we could all just show compassion and understanding. Some people just need an ear to listen. Some need a sincere "How was your day?" Others need someone they can trust to open up to. Sometimes people just need to be valued and feel they are worthy of love. Some are hurting inside with no way of releasing that hurt and for that they will always ask, "What did I do?" A little compassion in relationships, both friendship and intimate, goes a long way. Maybe it could help to begin healing the anxiety so much of society feels, the loneliness that many experience, and quite possibly the generational abuse cycles. Mental and emotional health are just as important as your physical health. If you are feeling anxious, depressed, defeated, and not engaged in life-you may need to examine your environment to make the necessary changes for your mental well-being. Understand that change is hard to make, but we all deserve to be happy and healthy. Someone cannot make those choices for you, but a little encouragement and support go a long way to help others. Find and be around people that lift you up and bring good energy. Often, if you choose to develop the qualities in yourself that you seek in others, you will begin to attract those relationships. It's tough at times, but dig deep internally to heal yourself. Discover what may trigger the anxiety, or what situations make you sad. Then, learn to avoid the triggers and make different choices.

My dad had a rough childhood. He was not raised by his parents, but by his grandparents. He lost his brother at a young age and had to grow up well before his youth was over. He lacked love, compassion, and that family bond. I do not blame him for not knowing what a normal relationship and family should be like because he did not have one modeled for him.

I went down this same road with relationships throughout my life; it took a divorce to heal my brokenness. I finally made the decision one day that we were better off divorced and being friends than we were staying married and continuing to show our girls what an unhealthy relationship looks like.

I found the courage to break the cycle, and you can too. Step back if you are in an unhealthy relationship and ask yourself if you would want a man to treat your little girl the way you are being treated. You will know the answer. If you are in that situation, know that you have the God-given strength inside to ensure the cycle ends with you. It's important that your children see a strong mom being treated well, for them to learn what kind of behavior is acceptable, and witness what should not tolerated in a relationship.

It's so much better to have a family where a little girl learns from her strong mother how to be a great wife and a little boy can learn from a gentle father how to be a wonderful husband, than to live in a home where all their little eyes pick up is an unhealthy relationship.

Some people are lessons and a test from the universe, see them for that and move on. I personally have had some hard lessons—ones I hope you don't have to learn. Please know when you are presented with the lesson, learn it the first time, or it will be repeated again until you finally get it. Forget what hurt you in the past, but never forget what it taught you. Perhaps the best revenge you can ever have in life is growth. Mind your business and look inside to grow yourself when you've been hurt by someone. Remember to offer them grace because you do not know the inner demons that person is dealing with. Say prayers for them and move on. We all get what we tolerate. It's important that you make sure what you are tolerating is healthy, loving, and kind. If you want drama in your life, go watch Netflix.

Be ok with the divorce if it is necessary for your health and that of your children. Be strong enough to walk on your own and not rely on someone else. A very important lesson and rule is: always be more than capable of doing life on your own. You can do anything you set your mind to, as my momma would say. I'm thankful she instilled this in me at such a young age, so that I knew that I could take those stones that were thrown at me, pick them up, and build something great. Be strong, independent, and accomplish your dreams; I promise there will be a day the right man will want to be with you by your side in life. Do not dumb yourself down or belittle yourself so that you are not too much for him. If people make you feel like you are too much, those are not your people. God created an incredible you to shine bright, be bold, and show the world what's possible. If you love yourself, you will not cling to a relationship trying to get love from a man who doesn't love you back. The right man will love you for all the right reasons and will celebrate your uniqueness.

I so wish I had a crystal ball to tell you how it will end or some pixie dust to create the perfect Prince Charming to pick you up in a carriage and treat you like the princess you are. I would love to tell you there won't be any frogs to kiss before he finally arrives. Unfortunately, the best I can tell you is God has a plan and the right man for you one day. There will be heartache and heartbreak, but don't you dare waste your tears on a guy who doesn't appreciate your value! You bring way too much to the table, and I know you aren't afraid to eat alone.

Be with the guy who isn't afraid to carry your purse. The one who likes to show you off. The one who makes you cry from laughter. Be with the one who holds your hand, listens to you talk about your day, and holds you when you are at your lowest. Be with someone who knows how you like your coffee, who does the dishes out of the blue, and surprises you by having the laundry folded when you forget it. Find the man who is ready to tackle life with you, who can withstand your hardest days, and who is ready to build a strong foundation with you. Make sure he opens your door, walks on the outer side of the curb, and pulls out your chair. It sounds simple, but a true gentleman will always treat you as the queen you are. The man who brings home the $5 flowers for no reason or the little notes that make you smile just knowing you were thought of has the right intentions. Be with your best friend, the man who makes you smile and is there by your side through it all.

It's the little things they do when they go out of their way to make you feel special that mean the most. Like one night while I was at the grocery store, I noticed a young guy with a printed recipe intently shopping. I could hear him an aisle over asking a store employee if there's a difference between crushed and minced garlic. Not knowing the answer, the lady radioed to see if someone else could help. As I rounded the corner, the two of them were standing in the middle of the aisle, staring at a jar of garlic. The young man looked so stressed, I couldn't help but ask what he was making to see if I could help. He said he would be making lasagna for Sunday night dinner. I asked if he was making the spaghetti sauce for the lasagna from scratch, and he said yes while referring to the multiple printouts and directions that were all bunched up in his hands. I told him to head to produce and get some fresh garlic. He was excited to have gotten a little direction.

I'm not a cook by any means, but I know fresh is always best. The young man explained he was grateful for my recommendation because he wanted this to be a really special dinner. I didn't ask questions but told him to make the sauce when he got home and let it simmer, then cook the lasagna the next night when he was ready to make dinner. He seemed excited and happy as he turned and headed toward produce.

A little while later, I saw him at the checkout. I didn't see everything in his basket, but I did notice two things that really made me pause and think. He bought a candelabrum for the table and white candles to go in it. He had the biggest smile, and I thought, *Wow, he's so excited to make someone a special dinner, and he even thought of a centerpiece for the ambience.* I almost shouted out, "Did you grab fresh baked Italian bread to make garlic bread?" but I held back because I didn't want to make him any more stressed. He clearly was going the extra mile to impress someone.

Crossing his path at the store that day made me realize that there are still men out there who want to impress and do make the effort—men who go the extra mile to make you feel special when they really, truly care about you. Chivalry is not completely lost. I still wonder how that dinner went for him, if they are together in a relationship, and if the lasagna was awesome with that fresh garlic!

It's the little things that will add up later in life. It's what memories are made of. Never get too busy with life that you don't have time for the other person to be able to grow together. Make time for the moments that will leave an impression on your heart. Those memories will live with you forever. Life is about more than your to-do lists, calendars, and schedules. Be open to having the love of your life show up when you are ready, and the time is right. You should successfully master being *you* first; don't settle, and don't change just to fit someone else's ideal. Learn to love yourself. Be, without a doubt, like who you want to attract, and the universe will deliver him to your doorstep—just like the universe did for me.

LAYING LOW AND ACCEPTING THE STATUS QUO IS NOT OKAY-EVER!

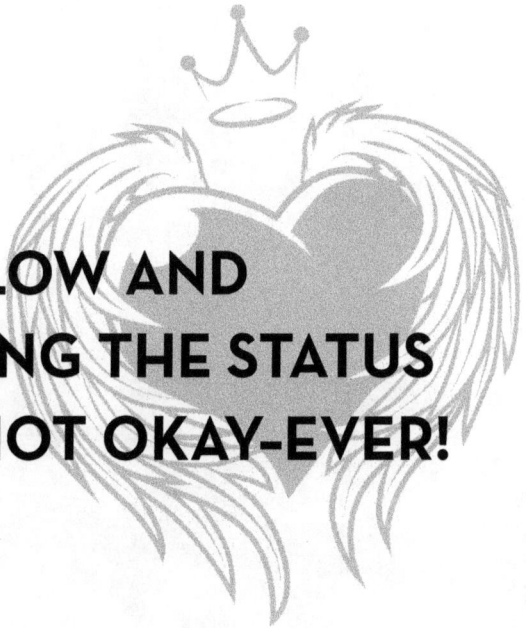

There's nothing worse than a stagnant life. When you are stuck, you are missing out on what life has in store for you. When you are not growing, you are dying. Please tell me you wouldn't want to live the same day on repeat for the next one, five, or ten years of your life. Living life as if you are walking around in a fog—too focused on where you've been and what's happened to you to consider where you want to go.

Take it from me, I lived this way for a few years after my divorce. I was just trying to cope. I kept to myself; I isolated from those around me. The end of my marriage felt like I had failed. I thought people were against me, that they were unhappy with me for choosing to end the marriage. At that time, I was too focused on my past and what was happening to me to look ahead to see what was new. I was in a fog and clearly taking the easy road with many aspects of my life. My work was on cruise control, as I had done it for so many years and could do it most days with my eyes closed. My home was easy and comfortable, but not the home my girls and I wanted. My health and gym routine were getting back in gear. Life was ordinary and secure. I was afraid to do much else as I was barely putting the pieces back together to heal myself after the seven long years of marriage.

But, it's in these times, in the midst of the sheltered life you're living, that you should look for ways to change that will take you to the next level. Let the pain from failure drive you to success. It's through change that we grow. You don't need to make big changes; sometimes small changes are what we can handle at the time, but they add up to larger changes over time. That's where growth is found. There is no need to shrink yourself down in life or hide behind the wall that you've put up. What are you hiding behind and why are you accepting 'average'? It's time to show yourself to the world even though some things may scare you, because you are missing out on God's plan and purpose for your life by not using your gifts.

Your life and gifts are like none other. You are special and have a unique purpose. God wants you to have an abundant and fulfilled life, and the status quo will not get you there. Step out into the unknown and allow the universe to gift you with a big and full life. Overcome your fears and don't ever live a life that is ordinary. You don't get a do over in life, so live it with no regrets.

See how life changes when you let go of what you think is safe, stable, and responsible in order to open up and allow the possibilities that God has in store! I can't promise they will all be good days. There will be hard days... like, really hard. I'm reminded of a day I picked my girls up, stopped at two grocery stores, got gas (didn't I just get gas Saturday?), went home, unloaded the groceries, unpacked lunch boxes, put groceries away, started dinner—had to empty the dishwasher first—then fed the hungry dogs whining at me, started dinner (again), went to put my sheets in the dryer (so I can finally sleep when I'm ready!), but had to fold the clothes in the dryer first. Meanwhile, Charley was sucked into her iPod and Dani was outside with sidewalk chalk drawing. I only know what Dani was doing because she came in like three times asking me to come out and look at her picture. My response—"In a minute, I'm trying to get your dinner ready because you said you were hungry. In a minute, I'm in the middle of feeding the dogs. Almost, I'm putting the sheets in the dryer." She finally got mad at me and stomped up the stairs.

Feeling like my best just somehow always falls short and needing a breather for a minute, I stepped outside to find her chalk drawing. I broke down in tears and was totally reminded of my "WHY." Her drawing read, "You are the Best Mom Ever" surrounded by a big heart. After my hard and exhausting day, her words made me smile and remember that even on the tough days, it's all worth it for my girls. They are my world.

Not all days are easy. Not all days are happy. Everything doesn't fall into place every time. But somehow it all works out and gets done. This hard, single mom life will always have its ups and downs, but I wouldn't trade my two girls for anything. I'm not the first, nor will I be the last single mom, I will always do my best to raise strong daughters who are able to make it through life on their own and one day without me. Until then, I just need to breathe and let the hard days go, knowing tomorrow is another chance to get it right.

Never give up on yourself, your dreams, and your passions. Fix, heal, and grow so you can be the strong mom God made you to be. Raise those babies and break the cycles, because you—and they—deserve so much more. The cycles can be abuse, depression, divorce, obesity, or poverty, just to name a few. We all have our struggles, remember? God gives us grace and faith; use your grit to get through the hard times. No matter how hard you push or how tired you seem to be, you need to dig deep and only play big in life. Laying low and the status quo will get you the same life every day. Go live this amazing life you've been blessed with, find your purpose, and chase it with all your heart. You need to take massive action to kickstart your way, especially when attacking the things that scare you. When you do the things that scare you, they will eventually become habits where fear no longer lives. It will then be time to level up once again.

Coming from a bad marriage, separation, and—finally— divorce, the struggle was all too real. Trying to hold it all together when life seemed to be falling apart was the hardest thing to do. Through all of the heartache, the truths revealed, and learning how to be a single mom, I had one simple goal every day: to always do what was best for my girls. That perspective kept me on the right path for my family, my girls, and my healing. They did not choose who I married. They weren't responsible for the problems in our marriage. They did not choose to have divorced parents. Those choices were made by others. So now it was time for me to choose well for them. I choose to be a strong role model for them. I will choose what is best for them over what I want any day of my life.

Not everyone sees inside your world and what you are dealing with, but they will see how you face your problems with strength, dignity, and respect. Be the strong role model as a Strong Mom raising Stronger Daughters. Fall in love with yourself every day. Learn to focus on yourself, build yourself up, raise your price and your value to bring abundance into your life. You will attract what is ready to show up in your life, but only when you are ready to show up for yourself. Find those people who inspire you to be better, to do great things; surround yourself with those who motivate you, who hold you accountable. Those are your people. There are strong women who will teach you the lessons they have already learned from the hard times they have fought through. They will be your strength when you need it most, helping you to know there is a way through and that you are not the first to face such obstacles.

In *The Wizard of Oz*, Glenda the Good Witch tells Dorothy, "You had the power all along, my dear." Like Dorothy, you need to realize and know that every girl has a voice that can change the world. Just be brave enough to share it. Fight past the fear to achieve your goals and dreams. Be intentional and persistent in pursuing the life you manifest, and along the way the co-inky-dinks will have you smiling as the universe winks at you.

Be thankful every day for the blessings and abundances in your life. Remember to pray and pull strength from God when you need it and be open to allowing him to take control. Enjoy the little moments–they will sometimes be the biggest memories later. Let go and let God radically transform your life, your family, and your relationships.

My life has evolved so much over the last 36 months! I'm so grateful I stepped into the possibilities, opened up to what life has to offer, and let go of my agenda. I'm beyond thankful for the path God has taken me down–a path I couldn't imagine or plan myself and better than I ever thought possible. I look forward to the months and years to come when I am helping others see what's possible, focusing on the blessings, being mindful of the little things, enjoying every moment, and living the big, full life that God has planned.

What is stopping you? Now is the perfect time to slow down and listen to that inner voice. What do you want to do? What changes do you need to make, what has to give, or what do you have to give up in your life? What are the things you need to let go of to allow God to show you the possibilities? I can tell you from experience, when you have faith in him to guide you along your path, he has a better plan than you can imagine. He will show you what is possible when you put your trust in him. You have a choice with how you handle fear; you can either face everything and rise or forget everything and run. What's your choice?

Don't let your life be governed by fear. I want to live the most abundant life God has in store for me. I know he's got my back and when the fear hits, I let go and let God. Don't let fear be the reason you don't do things. If you allow fear to stop you, it will keep showing up again and again, and prevent you from doing other things. Fear is a liar. *Feel the fear and do it anyway!* (By the way, that book, written by Susan Jeffers, is great too.)

What do you fear? Whatever it is, tackle it; that's where you will find the most growth in your life! Trust me, and just like I did, let go and let God. He's got very big plans for your life–bigger than you could imagine!

My best advice is: do not be anxious, do not fear, do not worry. Let faith be your guide. Constantly remind yourself that God will provide in your time of need. He will be there for you when you feel alone and begin to question what you are doing. If you are intentional about your days, you won't need to question what you're doing. If you remember to take the time to plan and prepare your days focusing on those dreams and goals, you will know you are on the right path. If you are not happy and hate what you are doing, then it may be time to do the things you fear. Sit still and have a quiet conversation with that inner voice. Let him know what you need and where you feel empty. Ask for God's guidance and be ready when he shows up in your life! It's time to feel the fear and do it anyway. It's time to be that Strong Mom raising up Stronger Daughters in this crazy life. Show every girl and woman that their voice can change the world. I truly believe what my Aunt Vickie said (and lived) and I hold it to be true in my life, too: Go big or go home! Be a badass, create the most magnificent life imaginable and show those around you what is possible.

Sherri was raised in a small southern Maryland town. Having grown up in a one traffic light, rural town, she wanted to go away to attend college in a larger city. At nineteen, she headed south to Florida on her own. This was the best decision she could have made as the experiences helped shape her life and some major lessons were realized. At twenty-seven, Sherri headed back north to that small coastal town to be close to her parents, which again turned out to be a life-changing decision. Nothing is ever a coincidence, and when you begin to realize there is a path and purpose, the guidance to lead you where you need to be is ever apparent.

Sherri, a single mom of two amazing girls, now lives just outside that small town that's not so small anymore. As an only child, she's thrilled to be closer than ever to her mother. Her mission is to show her daughters and all young women that their voices can change the world. Women should be taught valuable lessons by the strong women near them who have already gone through the struggles – Strong women raising up the women around them as stronger daughters. It's time to believe in yourself.

If you have a testimony of a strong woman in your life who showed you what belief in yourself can do, or if you have your own experience of lessons learned, please reach out to share your story. We can all learn and benefit from each other. Strong moms and stronger daughters need to show the world that women should raise each other up, lifting those who are struggling so they know it's all possible. Be that fierce woman in pursuit of your path, passion, purpose, and happiness.

✉: sherri@strongmomstrongerdaughters.com
💻: www.strongmomstrongerdaughters.com
⬡: @strongmomstrongerdaughters

scan me

Every woman's success should be an inspiration to another.
We're strongest when we cheer each other on
– Serena Williams

www.ingramcontent.com/pod-product-compliance
Lightning Source LLC
Chambersburg PA
CBHW070123100426
42744CB00010B/1905